FESTIVAL OF FIRE
Series No. 3

GOD'S AGENT OF REVIVAL

The Heart of a Catalyst of Revival

Godson T. Nembo

GOD'S AGENT OF REVIVAL:
The Heart of a Catalyst of Revival

Copyright © September 2023
Godson T. Nembo

All rights reserved.
ISBN : 978-1-63603-192-7

Published in Cameroon by
Christian Restoration Network (CRN) Publications
P.O. BOX 31339 Yaounde – Cameroon

IEM PRESS is honored to present this title with the author. The views expressed or implied in this work are those of the author. IEM Press provides our imprint seal representing design excellence, creative content and high quality production. To learn more about IEM Press visit www.iempublishing.com

No part of this publication may be reproduced, stored in a retrieval system, or transmitted in any way by any means—electronic, mechanical, photocopy, recording, or otherwise—without the prior permission of the copyright holder, except as provided by USA copyright law.

All scripture quotations are from the New King James Version (NKJV) of the Bible, except otherwise stated.

For more information:
www.christianrestorationnetwork.org
www.facebook.com/godsontnembo
Email: contact@christianrestorationnetwork.org

Or write to:
Tangumonkem Godson Nembo
P.O. Box 31339 Biyem Assi Yaounde – Cameroon
Tel: (237) 652.382.693 or 696.565.864

Prayer Storm Online Store:
With MTN or Orange Mobile Money *(for those in Cameroon)* and E-Wallet *(for those abroad)*, you can easily obtain the electronic version of this book and other CRN publications via www.amazon.com at
https://shorturl.at/pqxyT or
www.christianrestorationnetwork.org/our-bookstore.
https://goo.gl/ktf3rT
Contact (237) 679.465.717 or
prayerstorm@christianrestorationnetwork.org

Cover Design: Tangu Monkem (237) 671.331.222
Layout: IEM Press (237) 672.827.784

How to Use this Book

Carefully read these instructions before you start praying with this book.
1) **Read the message of the day** and all the scriptures before you start praying.
2) **Use the prayer points provided at the end of each chapter as a guide,** but depend on the Holy Spirit to reveal more.
3) **Pray all the prayers audibly** and not in your heart. Don't disturb anybody.
4) **Take time and pray through each prayer point before you move** to the next one.
5) **If you can, always pray in tongues** as you pray with this book.
6) **Pause and listen to God** as you pray because He has many things to reveal to you.
7) **If you are following the 30 days program, read and pray with each chapter for 3 days.** Divide the prayer points as you wish.
8) **Write down your prayer topics** to pray during the fast.
9) **As led by the Holy Spirit, you can also select topics** from this book to carry out a 1 day, 3 days, 7 days, 21 days, or even 40 days fast.
10) Pastors, prayer cell leaders, ministry heads, etc., can use this book to lead their Churches or groups for a season of fasting and prayer.
11) **You can still pray without fasting** if your health condition does not permit you to fast now.

Practical Rules for Fasting
Read through and apply these rules if you have decided to fast with this book:

1) **Consecrate yourself.** This is because a sinner's prayer is an abomination before God (1 Peter 3:12).
2) **Except otherwise, break the fast every evening after 6 pm** and continue the next day.
3) **Decide how many days you want to fast** to avoid being discouraged along the journey.

4) *Drink water ONLY during the day, as you fast.* No fruits, no fruit juice, no tea, no coffee, no soft drinks, and no candies should be taken. Experts say our daily intake of water should be at least 8 glasses (250 ml).
5) *Spend much time praying*, reading, and studying the messages in this book and also your Bible.
6) *BREAK THE FAST EVERY EVENING WITH A LOT OF CARE.*
    - Begin with lukewarm water or pressed fruit juice (watermelon, mango, pineapple, pawpaw, cucumber, beetroot, carrot, etc.).
    - Eat a plate of salad (do not use mayonnaise for salad cream instead mix honey, olive oil, and lemon juice or apple cider vinegar, and use as cream).
    - Then eat some cooked food (eat raw food first before you take in any cooked food).
    - If possible, eat more raw food during your fast.
    - Don't overeat or mix many different types of foods (even fruits).
7) *Foods to eliminate during your fast:*
    - For the enhancement of the process of proper body detoxification and self-healing, eliminate the following foods from your diet during the fast:
        a) MSG, generally found in Maggi cubes, agino moto, etc. (Eat without Maggi; use just salt, if possible sea salt).
        b) Any type of sugar (use only pure and natural honey).
        c) Artificial sweeteners (do not use aspartame, saccharin, sucralose, etc.).
        d) Fried foods (do not fry fish, meat, plantains, potatoes, etc.).
        e) Eat mostly whole wheat bread.
        f) Refined oils (eat only soya beans oil, sunflower oil, palm oil, or olive oil).
8) *Don't engage in excessive work or exercises* during the fast. You can exercise for 30 minutes, three times a week (you can just walk and stretch).
9) *Write down the things the Holy Spirit reveals to you:* dreams, inspirations, songs, and prophecies. You may lose them if you don't do so.

How to Use this Book

10) ***Settle any dispute you have*** with somebody before you start fasting. It can block your prayer. Avoid quarrels and arguments during and after the fast.

11) ***Don't focus on the body's weaknesses*** – the body is just reacting to the absence of food. Keep telling yourself, "It is well; I am an eagle, and I will make it to the end!"

12) ***Pray with expectation.*** God will never let you seek Him in vain.

13) ***Make sacrifices*** (gifts) during and after your fast. Prepare a special thanksgiving offering to present to the Lord at the end of the fast.

14) ***In case you have any difficulty***, meet your spiritual leader or someone who is experienced in fasting.

15) ***Regarding sex during a fast***, the Bible says:

   "Do not refuse to give your bodies to each other unless you both agree to stay away from sexual relations for a time so you can give your time to prayer. Then come together again so Satan cannot tempt you because of a lack of self-control" (1 Corinthians 7:5) NCV.

I hope you know that all sexual relationships out of marriage are sinful; before, during, and after the fast? It is not sinful for a married couple to have sex during a fast when the two are in agreement. Sex between MARRIED couples does not defile a fast. It is wrong to deprive your spouse without their consent. It is best to stay away from sex to focus your energy on seeking the Lord. Let the Holy Spirit guide you in everything.

16) ***Don't pray only for yourself***; pray for other people as well as the nation. Ask the Holy Spirit to reveal urgent issues that need prayer to you.

17) ***Saturate your life with praise and worship.*** Sing and also listen to anointed gospel music every day. This will create a conducive atmosphere around your life for the move of the Holy Spirit.

Table of Contents

How to Use this Book v

Introduction 11

Chapter 1: **A New Heart** 17
Days 1-3

Chapter 2: **A Heart Hungry for God** 37
Days 4-6

Chapter 3: **A Broken Heart** 53
Days 7-9

Chapter 4: **A Thankful Heart** 69
Days 10-12

Chapter 5: **A Heart Full of Love** 81
Days 13-15

Chapter 6: **A Heart Full of Faith** 97
Days 16-18

Chapter 7: **A Faithful Heart** 115
Days 19-21

Chapter 8: **A Patient Heart** 131
Days 22-24

Chapter 9: **A Merciful Heart** 145
Days 25-27

Chapter 10: **A Courageous Heart** 159
Days 28-30

Conclusion 175

The Restoration House Project 175

Endnotes 176

Introduction

God accomplishes unimaginable works in every generation through useable and available human instruments. He lavishly reveals His love, power, and glory whenever He finds Kingdom-minded people. Hence, spiritual darkness is not the absence of God; it is the lack of men and women light. Sin and wickedness triumph only where the righteous are absent. Injustice and corruption prevail only when people of integrity are non-existent. Satan and his agents dominate only where men and women of fire are scarce.

Cognizant of man's strategic role in every Kingdom venture on earth, God constantly begins His projects in the heart. He does so because there is no way you can change and use a man without conquering his heart. Therefore, "God's Agent of Revival" discussed in this book is one in whose heart God is doing a profound work and is being used as an instrument for Kingdom expansion. When God takes over our hearts, our heads (minds) and hands become tools for divine transformation and impact. Thus, the world's greatest need at this time is men and women whose hearts are passionate for God and compassionate for man. People passionate about God want to do His will and see His name glorified at all costs. In the same light, compassionate people are willing to pay any price for the salvation and the restoration of man's dignity. These are the people God is searching for as catalysts of revival and restoration.

What is Revival?
Let me begin with what revival is not:
(1) Revival is not a set of church meetings. We often say, "We have three days of revival meetings or a revival program". Revival can happen during a meeting, but naming a church meeting "A revival meeting" does not guarantee a revival.
(2) Revival is not a crusade. The salvation of several souls in an evangelistic meeting may not be a revival.
(3) The numerical growth of a church may not be a revival. Several factors draw people to the Church.

(4) Revival is not noise. Often, churches invite preachers who shout and stir the audience during revival programs. The charismatic preacher's noise may shake people physically and emotionally but not change them spiritually.
(5) Revival is not a display of fascinating prophecies. Prophecies and mind-blowing revelations of hidden things in people's lives may not be a revival. We have noticed that often, after such crowd-pulling programs, the status quo remains unchanged – no transformation in the Church and society.
(6) Revival is not a significant offering collected. Sometimes, people are motivated to give their all not by the touch of the Holy Spirit but by the motivational skill of the preacher.
(7) Revival is not a big concert. Talented professional artists can pull crowds and stir them to tears without impacting them spiritually. Sadly, people who wept during the show continue in their sinful ways afterward as if nothing had happened to them.

What, then, is revival?

"Revival" combines two Latin words, *'Vivo,'* meaning to live, and *'Re'* meaning again. It's like a rebirth or a re-awakening where the Holy Spirit moves freely among believers, setting their hearts on fire for the Lord.[1]

"Revival" is like a river that goes out of the church building, spills out to the streets, spreads all over the arterial roads, and eventually saturates the whole city with the Gospel of Jesus Christ.[2]

Some definitions by various authors:

- "God's quickening visitation of his people, touching their hearts and deepening his work of grace in their lives" (J. I. Packer).
- "The sovereign act of God, in which He restores His own backsliding people to repentance, faith, and obedience" (Stephen Olford).
- "Times of refreshing from the presence of the Lord" (Acts 3:19) J. Edwin Orr.
- "The awakening or quickening of God's people to their true nature and purpose" (Robert Coleman).
- "The return of the Church from her backslidings, and the conversion of sinners" (Charles Finney).

- "An extraordinary movement of the Holy Spirit producing extraordinary results" (Richard Owen Roberts).
- "A community saturated with God" (Duncan Campbell).
- "The work of the Holy Spirit in restoring the people of God to a more vital spiritual life, witness, and work by prayer and the Word after repentance in crisis for their spiritual decline" (Earle Cairns).

Experts say:
- It is a RENEWAL when God touches the heart of a single individual.
- It is a REVIVAL when God touches a community.
- It is an AWAKENING when the wider society is impacted.[3]

What are the Conditions for a Revival?
Certain things MUST happen before a revival:
(1) A burning thirst for holiness, accompanied by sincere profound repentance and restitution.
(2) Commitment to Christ-centered kingdom expansion prayers.
(3) An earnest desire to manifest God's power for signs and wonders.
(4) A burning love for God and compassion for His people.
(5) Christ-entered preaching (The Gospel of the Kingdom).
(6) Aggressive engagement in evangelization, discipleship, church planting, and missions.

Peculiarities of a Revival
(1) *Revival is intentional.* We receive it through transforming our deep desire for God into moments of intensive personal and corporate soul-searching prayers.
(2) *Revival is personal.* The revival fire in a church begins with individuals.
(3) *Revival is purifying.* Every genuine revival changes man's wicked and crooked heart.
(4) *Revival results in prioritizing God.* Believers become vigorously involved in God's worship and His work.
(5) *Revival draws multitudes of sinners to Christ.*

Some Examples of Revivals

1) *The Day of Pentecost:*

An excellent example of a revival is what happened on the Day of Pentecost. The Holy Spirit baptized one and twenty believers in the Upper Room, and their preaching became contagious, drawing three thousand souls to Christ that day (Acts 2). Multitudes continue to believe the Gospel as the Church grew from Jerusalem to the ends of the earth within a few decades.

2) *The revival in Wales:*

In 1904, a young ministerial student named Evan Roberts began to feel that God was sending an urgent message that He would pour out a mighty spirit of revival on Wales, which is now a part of Great Britain. Roberts began attending various revival meetings, and during one, he was deeply moved by the Spirit. As he prayed at the altar, he cried out to God, "Bend me o Lord!" This was a complete and total surrender of his will to God's will.

After praying, reading, and preaching on revival for thirteen years, Evan Roberts spoke in a church for nearly two hours, with a simple four-point message that he was convinced could help God bring revival. (1) Confess all known sins to God. (2) Deal with and eliminate any "doubtful" area of your life. (3) Be ready to obey the Holy Spirit instantly. (4) Confess Christ publicly.

When Roberts was finished speaking, seventeen young people were at the altar on their knees, crying out to God. They prayed until 2 a.m. that night, and it was the beginning of one of the most significant movements of God in all history. By the end of the week, over sixty people were won to Christ, and revival swept through the nation of Wales throughout the next one and a half years. Over one hundred thousand people were led to saving faith in Jesus Christ. The fire spread beyond Wales and led to the conversion of over one million people.

The revival was so great that the national culture changed dramatically.

- A rage of bankruptcies took place. All of the taverns and liquor stores went out of business.
- Work at the coal mines was brought to a near standstill. The mules who pulled the wagons were so accustomed

to hearing foul language from the workers that they no longer recognized their voices or commands after the men were saved.
- The entire police force was dismissed for almost 18 months due to a complete lack of crime.
- One of the few court cases that was actually brought before a judge was unusual. The defendant came into the court and admitted his guilt, the judge led the man to Christ, and the jury closed the case by singing a hymn.

3) *The revival in Northampton:*

Jonathan Edwards fasted and prayed for three days; it was an absolute fast with no food or water. He wanted the unsaved in his Church to be converted. Around 4:00 on Sunday afternoon, Edwards began to choke and gag. He violated his fast by drinking water. He was not supposed to end his fast until sundown on Sunday. That evening, he went into the pulpit, a broken man. With a lantern in one hand and a manuscript in another, he read the sermon, "Sinner In The Hands of An Angry God." The power of God fell on that sermon, and men grabbed the pillars for fear of slipping into Hell.

Parts of that sermon were powerful and graphic. Jonathan Edwards said, "You are a worm hanging over the precipice of Hell. The flames are licking at the spider web, and at any moment, you may drop into eternal damnation." As members felt dangling over Hell, they cried out in repentance. That evening, the First Great Awakening began in Massachusetts and spread throughout the thirteen colonies. Later, Edwards wrote a pamphlet entitled The Surprising Work of God in Northampton to report the revival.

4) *God's move in Africa:*

Rick Joyner wrote in *Morning Star Prophetic Bulletin*, "Revival, renewal, awakening--none of these words seem big enough to describe what is currently happening in Africa. Entire regions are radically impacted by the Gospel, and whole cities are falling to their knees, confessing Jesus as Lord. Looking at the numbers, there is nothing in history to compare with the present move of God in Africa. One African newspaper reported last year that 'Africa is Being Saved.'"[4]

God Wants to Do it Again

Most of our communities are ripe for revival. God is looking for a catalyst to activate the fire. I believe this book is in your hands because God has chosen you to be one of those He will use this season. He wants to prepare you; that is why this book focuses on "The Heart of a Catalyst of Revival." The Holy Spirit will do a profound work of transformation in your life as you open your heart fully to Him.

The Church does not need more programs or more events. We desperately need an outpouring of the Holy Spirit. We urgently need God to come and change our hearts. Only Him can change our hearts. That is why we have to fast and surrender to Him.

God has poured out His Spirit in several places across Church history. He will do it again in our midst. This is the time to seek Him until He opens the heavens over us and pours out His fire and rain for our transformation and blessing.

Written as a guide for the 23rd edition of the annual 30-day fast, organized by the Christian Restoration Network (CRN), this work is an incredible tool to equip you to become a catalyst of revival in your family, Church, community, and nation. It will guide you through an unforgettable experience in God's presence.

God bless you as you use this book to pray with us and multitudes of believers across the globe.

Pastor Godson T. Nembo
Pretoria, South Africa
September 6, 2023

Introduction

Chapter 1
Days 1-3

A New Heart

"I will give you a new heart and put a new spirit within you; I will take the heart of stone out of your flesh and give you a heart of flesh" (Ezekiel 36:26).

The heart of a regenerated believer is a platform for the multidimensional operations of God. I was privileged to be raised by God-fearing parents who modeled Christ to me. The impact of their faith in my life is indescribable.

Mom returned from the annual women's retreat organized by the Full Gospel Mission Cameroon Women's Ministry in Bamenda that year, with a burning enthusiasm to see her family move to a brand-new level. She immediately went to work! The first thing was to convince my dad to acquire a new dining table and a set of chairs, to enable our family to eat together. This was one of the new lessons she had learned during the retreat – "A family that prays together and eats together stays strong together."

Even though we prayed and fed from God's Word every morning as a family, the norm was that Daddy's food was served on the lone small table in the house. He ate alone while the kids ate together on the floor, either in the kitchen or parlor. I cannot figure out where Mom used to eat her food; maybe in her kitchen.

Thank God for Daddy. He immediately ordered a dining table with eight chairs to be fabricated. I don't know how he squeezed himself to pay for the furniture, considering that only a portion of his salary as a Grade Two Teacher was reaching him then. When the new furniture was finally brought in, Mom had a great surprise for us – salad! We had never heard about salad, which was not part of our family menu in a remote village then.

That evening, for the first time, we sat on the new chairs, anxiously waiting for Mom to serve our plates with the salad she had prepared from the cabbage and other ingredients. All of us ate the salad with excitement. We found it so delicious, unlike some kids who would reject a new dish, especially when it is raw vegetables. One thing that fanned our appetite was that the salad was a new dish Mama had learned during the retreat to prepare for her family. Interestingly, she served us salad whenever she could get the vegetables and other ingredients. This was a great sacrifice on her part because we lived in a village where vegetables like cabbages, tomatoes, carrots, green beans, and the rest were not grown. It required much effort to lay hands on those items.

Mom's love for Jesus Christ and her zeal to practice God's Word ushered us into a new dimension of life. We were now eating together at the table as a family, which was rare in that village then. I felt I was a special boy, thanks to the Gospel of Jesus Christ.

The Only Giant Bible in the Village

The next surprise came during another church program my parents traveled from the village to Bamenda to attend. They were taught the importance of exposing infants to God's Word early, through picture Bibles. They immediately invested money and bought a giant pictorial Bible for us. There was none like it in the whole village. Throughout my life, I have scarcely seen such a big Bible in families. Coming at a time when there was no TV set in the entire village, children began conglomerating in our home to watch the colorful pictures that accompanied the Bible stories. We spent hours each day during the holiday exploring one Bible story after the other. It is not an error that all of us are serving God today. My parents, motivated by God's love, invested in planting the seed of the Gospel in us early enough. Our love for Christ and His Word always leaves a profound impact on our families.

Not long ago, somebody who knew my family in that village, who had not seen me for over thirty years, said when he met me, "Godson, it is not a surprise that you became a pastor. You followed the footsteps of your parents." Why wouldn't I follow in my parent's footsteps when all I saw in them was the love and light of the Gospel? I saw how we were moved from grass to grace through God's mercy. I will serve Jesus Christ till the end.

How I Got Saved

My mother was the first to surrender her life to Jesus Christ in 1974, while my dad also came to Christ a year later. So, as a kid, I began following my parents to Full Gospel Mission church. I attended Sunday school, recited memory verses, and acted in drama but was not converted. I was just that calm church boy who looked like an angel outwardly but did not have Christ's life inside me. Around 1988, while in form two, in Seat of Wisdom College Fontem, a group of friends I had, who were older than me, introduced me to fornication and nasty life. I say, "They introduced me" because they took time to convince and manipulate me into it. They also introduced me to alcohol and smoking. I experienced firsthand what sociologists call "Peer pressure." The wrong environment can ruin a child's destiny.

While the devil was dragging me deeper into sin, my parents were restlessly bombarding the gates of Heaven for the salvation of my soul. At one point, their prayer topic was, "O Lord, let this young man hit the rock and turn to you." I always tell children who have consecrated and devoted Christian parents like mine that they are the most blessed children in the world.

On February 7, 1992, at about 7 pm, I was precisely at Mile 4 Junction, Nkwen Bamenda, Cameroon. A runaway Upper-Sixth student from CCAST Bambili roaming the streets of Bamenda. I had not taken a bath for more than one week. I was not mad per say, but busy with scammers, who had duped, and recruited me into their ranks. In answer to my parent's fervent prayers, God arrested me. God's power suddenly landed on my head that evening at that junction. I felt something I could not explain enter my heart, and I could hear Jesus Christ calling me to come to Him. I felt miserable as my sins and evil against my parents began to run through my mind. I began to weep profusely, asking God to show me mercy. Early the next day, like the prodigal son, I went back home to inform my parents of my decision to follow the Lord and ask them to forgive me for being such a nuisance.

The months that followed were fascinating as I pressed on in the faith. But unfortunately for me, I did not separate from my old friends. The devil used them to lure me back into my old sinful lifestyle. Everything went out of hand this time, and I went through hell for one year. Thank God in November 1993, I had a second encounter with Jesus that brought me back to the faith. On that day, I was in the house alone, and suddenly I felt an intense light around me, and God's presence was so tangible. I heard that voice that spoke to me the previous year calling me again. I wept for three hours, confessing and renouncing my sins. I decided to go to Church that Tuesday evening. I met an elder who prayed for me as I reconsecrated my life to Jesus Christ.

After this second encounter, I discovered that I could only go far in my walk with Jesus Christ with the baptism of the Holy Spirit. So, I began to fast every Wednesday to ask God for the experience. Praise God! On the 2nd of December 1993, the Holy Spirit came mightily upon me, and from that day, my life has never been the same again. I have been going from glory to glory by God's power, working wonders in and through my life. I received my call to the ministry the following year. God will do the same thing in your family as you pray for your children.

New Vessels Needed for New Wine

God's agents of revival are new vessels carrying the new wine of the Holy Spirit for generational transformation. There are many available vessels, but few are usable for God's work of revival. You may be busy in God's name but not fulfilling His will for your life. Your ministry may become famous, but you are not expanding God's Kingdom among men. Jesus said,

"But new wine is put into fresh wineskins, and so both are preserved" (Matthew 9:17 ESV).

Two things must happen to you to become a usable vessel in God's hands this season. First, you must be genuinely born again. Second, you must experience profound divine transformation. God must find space in you to fill and use you. He must take complete hold of you to use you. He must first shape you to send you.

The born-again and transformation experiences are divinely orchestrated but require your full collaboration.

You Must Be Born-Again

Even though indispensable for initiating a spiritual walk with Jesus Christ, some people naively criticize the concept of being "Born-again." They seem to insinuate that "Born-again" is the doctrine of a particular denomination and does not concern them. Did you know that Jesus Christ, the Master of the Church, introduced the concept in the New Testament?

> *"Jesus answered him, 'Truly, truly, I say to you, UNLESS ONE IS BORN AGAIN HE CANNOT see the kingdom of God" (John 3:3).*

Jesus is saying that there is no other way to become part of God's Kingdom apart from being born-again. Take this seriously!

What Does it Mean to be Born Again?

Being "Born again" is, a miracle of renewal produced by the Holy Spirit in someone's heart who has believed in Jesus Christ as the King of kings and Lord of lords. No human being can create the born-again experience. It is the sole work of the Holy Spirit. However, it requires man's willingness and collaboration.

> *"Jesus answered, 'Truly, truly, I say to you, unless one is born of water and the Spirit, he cannot enter the kingdom of God" (John 3:5).*

To become born-again begins with listening to the Gospel – the message of Jesus Christ as God's King who came to restore our victory over sin, Satan, the world, and suffering. Subsequently, one must go through the following steps to be genuinely born-again:

i. Admit that you are a sinner on your way to eternal damnation in hell.
ii. You must sincerely confess your sins and be willing to abandon them.
iii. You receive Jesus Christ into your heart by faith through a personal invitation.

iv. You must receive the forgiveness of your sins after confessing them by faith. Some people confess their sins but find it hard to believe they have been forgiven. They linger long under the weight of guilt.

> *"But if we confess our sins to him, he is faithful and just to forgive us our sins and to cleanse us from all wickedness" (1 John 1:9 NLT).*

i. You must receive God's love by faith. Some people find it hard to accept that God truly loves them. Maybe you have this problem because of the painful experiences you have gone through. 1 John 4:8-9 reveals that the coming of Jesus Christ manifested God's greatest love to us. We must accept it.

> *"God showed how much he loved us by sending his one and only Son into the world so that we might have eternal life through him. This is real love—not that we loved God, but that he loved us and sent his Son as a sacrifice to take away our sins (NLT).*

ii. You must agree that you are God's child by faith.

> *"But to all who believed him and accepted him, he gave the right to become children of God" (John 1:12 NLT).*

Your status changes when you receive Jesus Christ by faith. You must believe it.

iii. You must begin to follow Jesus Christ to learn from Him to become a true disciple.

> *"Then Jesus told his disciples, "If anyone would come after me, let him deny himself and take up his cross and follow me" (Matthew 16:24).*

Every genuinely born-again believer is following Jesus Christ as a disciple. If you are not following Him daily, you are not born-again or a disciple of Christ.

iv. You must abandon your sinful ways and join other believers serving God sincerely.

> *"Therefore, come out from among unbelievers, and separate yourselves from them, says the Lord. Don't touch their filthy things, and I will welcome you. And I will be your Father, and you will be my sons and daughters, says the Lord Almighty" (2 Corinthians 6:17-18 NLT).*

You cannot claim to be born again but still join unbelievers in their sinful practices. That is why Paul commanded the believers in Corinth to separate from ungodly associations with unbelievers.

Summarily, a born-again Christian is someone who has repented of their sins and has become a disciple (a follower) of Jesus Christ, and as a result, has become part of God's family forever. This work of grace occurs through the work of the Holy Spirit and the believer's faith.

Why must you be born again?

Let us look further into what Jesus Christ, the Master of the Church, said about being born-again to answer this critical question.

"Jesus answered and said to him, 'Most assuredly, I say to you, UNLESS ONE IS BORN AGAIN, HE CANNOT SEE THE KINGDOM OF GOD... Most assuredly, I say to you, unless one is born of water and the Spirit, he cannot enter the Kingdom of God. THAT WHICH IS BORN OF THE FLESH IS FLESH, and THAT WHICH IS BORN OF THE SPIRIT IS SPIRIT" (John 3:3, 5-6).

From this text, Jesus Christ brings out two eternal truths you must imbibe to establish your faith on a solid foundation.

1. *You must be born-again to be admitted into God's family:* Jesus underlines unequivocally that the gateway into God's family or Kingdom is the born-again experience.

   "I say to you, UNLESS ONE IS BORN AGAIN, HE CANNOT SEE THE KINGDOM OF GOD" (John 3:3).

Through the born-again experience, you receive God's life (DNA or spiritual genes) to become one of His sons or daughters. For instance, let us say you have a cat in your home you love so much, and you named it "Mimie." The truth is, the cat can never become one of your children, no matter how much you invest in training it. Why? Mimie belongs to a species utterly different from human beings. Cats cannot discuss nor do any business with human beings. The best Mimie can be in your home is to be your pet.

Now, one who is born again belongs to the species of "The spiritual family of God." While the one who is not born again like Mimie belongs to the species of "Natural human beings." Even though living in the same world, the two categories of human beings operate from two different realms and cannot flow together. They are on parallel lines, heading to two different destinations in eternity – Heaven or hell. You must be born-again to move from being just a natural man to the realm of a spiritual man.

Let me note that the born-again experience is not only for sinful or immoral people. Every human being must be born again to receive eternal life and become part of God's Kingdom or family. We have several people in Christian Churches who are not born again. They do not have Christ's life; consequently, they are not His Disciples. In fact, they don't have what it takes to live as His Disciples.

2. ***You can only develop or grow spiritually if you are born-again:*** In John 3:6, Jesus underlines that one must be born again as a prerequisite for spiritual development or growth. You must receive God's genes into your spirit before you can grow spiritually into a mature believer. Hence, copying spiritual things from regenerated people can ONLY make you spiritual when you are born again. Jesus said,

"That which is born of the flesh is flesh, and that which is born of the Spirit is spirit... (John 3:6).

He meant; natural human beings live in sin because that is how they have been wired. You don't have to teach a child born with a sinful nature to commit sins. The seed of evil in him develops and manifests as the child grows. Contrarily, one who is born again has God's life and, as such, develops progressively into a spiritual person who resembles Christ. In John 3:1-6, Jesus tells Nicodemus that the first step to spiritual growth is the born-again experience.

In the animal kingdom, a lizard resembles a crocodile, but they carry different genes. Consequently, a lizard can never grow into a crocodile, no matter how much you feed it. The simple reason is that the lizard does not carry the genes of a crocodile in its system. Similarly, an unregenerated church member can never become a spiritual person. A trained sinner can only become a religious person and not a saint (a Christ-like person). One not born by the Holy Spirit cannot become anything in God's Kingdom, no matter their ecclesiastical status or ranking in society.

Stop struggling to become a spiritual Christian. Receive Christ's life first. The power to become a true child of God is in Christ.

"But as many as received him, to them gave HE POWER TO BECOME THE SONS OF GOD, even to them that believe on his name" (John 1:12).

You must RECEIVE first; then, you can BECOME.

Are You Born Again?

Have you experienced the new birth of Christ Jesus? I am not talking about your denomination, ecclesiastical title, consecration into church service, or how long you have been in the Church. Remember what Jesus said to Nicodemus.

"I say to you, UNLESS ONE IS BORN AGAIN, HE CANNOT SEE THE KINGDOM OF GOD" (John 3:3).

Jesus' arms are wide open now to receive you into His Kingdom. You can experience the new birth now by believing that Jesus Christ is the King of kings and Lord of lords, who came and died on the cross to save you from sin, Satan, the world, and suffering. Confess your sins and invite Him now to come into your heart. Make up your mind to follow Him for the rest of your life. Do this before you continue if you have not yet decided to become a faithful follower of Jesus Christ. Kneel and pray this prayer:

> *"Dear Lord Jesus Christ, I believe You are King above all kings and Lord above all lords who came to save me from the power of sin, Satan, the world, and suffering. I believe that You have paid the full price for my freedom through Your death on the cross. Forgive my sins and cleanse me now. Give me a new heart. Fill me with Your Holy Spirit, and make me Your Disciple (Follower) from today. Set me free from every bondage, give me Your new life, and make me the person You want me to be, in Jesus' name."*

You Must Be Transformed

After you have been born again, your heart must be transformed to become an instrument of revival and restoration. An agent of revival needs a new heart through which God can work. God's pathway to manifesting His power among men is, the heart. Man's heart is His center of operations on earth at any moment. Therefore, God cannot move until He finds a useable heart. To obtain the quality of heart He can use in us, He passes us through different spiritual processes to produce profound transformation. Your role is to yield to the work of the Holy Spirit.

What is "Transformation?"

According to the Oxford English Dictionary, "Transformation" is "Thorough or dramatic change in form or experience". Spiritual transformation, is the process by which Christ is formed in us through the work of the Holy Spirit. Apostle Paul refers to this in Romans 12:2,

"Do not be conformed to this world, but be transformed by the renewal of your mind."

"Transformed" in this verse is Greek *'Metamorphoo,'* referring to the process by which a caterpillar enters into the darkness of a cocoon to emerge eventually changed, almost beyond recognition. The caterpillar transcends into a completely different creature – the butterfly through metamorphosis. This illustrates how the Holy Spirit transforms our lives into Christlikeness as we yield daily to Him.

The question you may ask is, "Is transformation possible? Can I truly change from evil to good? Or Can I truly be freed from this evil character in me?" The answer is an emphatic YES! The power released on the cross through Christ's death can change you if you are willing. I strongly agree with C. S. Lewis who said, "If we let Him – for we can prevent Him if we choose – He will make the feeblest and the filthiest of us into a dazzling, radiant, immortal creature, pulsating all through with such energy and joy and wisdom and love as we cannot now imagine…"

Are you hungry and thirsty for transformation? Do you desire to become like Christ in thinking, speaking, and acting? God will help you achieve it.

How Transformation Takes Place in Us

I have learned these spiritual truths about divine transformation during my thirty-one years of following Jesus Christ:

1. *Deep, Lasting Transformation is a Process:*

Profound transformation rarely happens overnight; we grow through a process into Christ-likeness – no shortcuts. It involves teaching, training, testing, and time. You cannot move from a spiritual babe into a mature believer through one long fast, impartation from a great man of God, or one long retreat. You grow progressively into maturity. Paul's prayer for the Galatians indicates he understood that Christlikeness is a process.

"Oh, my dear children! I feel as if I'm going through labor pains for you again, and they will continue UNTIL

CHRIST IS FULLY DEVELOPED IN YOUR LIVES" (Galatians 4:19 NLT).

You might have realized that as soon as you received Christ, you quickly threw off some works of the flesh from your life. Surprisingly, you may still be struggling with issues like anger, a lying tongue, pride, lust, food addiction, alcohol, etc. Don't give up! Change may take time, but it will surely come if you don't quit.

2. Spiritual Transformation Requires a Strong Desire:

We grow old naturally without furnishing any effort, but transformation does not happen like that. You must fervently desire it to experience it.

"Blessed are those who hunger and thirst for righteousness, For they shall be filled" (Matthew 5:6).

If you truly desire transformation, you will sincerely ask yourself these questions: (1) Do I really want change? Sadly, several people in the Church want healing and breakthroughs but are not interested in spiritual transformation. (2) Am I satisfied with my spiritual level or condition? Some folk want Jesus Christ but do not want to go far with Him. (3) What is God's purpose for my life? Am I pursuing it? (4) Am I willing to pay the price required for my transformation? Am I willing to let go from my life the things God hates? Without a strong desire, you cannot touch the fire of transformation.

3. Spiritual Transformation Flows From an Intimate Relationship With Jesus Christ:

Our deep love for Jesus Christ and constant fellowship with Him changes our nature. In 2 Corinthians 3:18, Paul points out that we are being transformed into the same image of Christ from glory to glory by the Spirit of God as we behold Jesus Christ continuously in His Word.

Also, we want to please those we love and are grieved when we offend them. The more we love Jesus, the greater will be our motivation to obey Him and to make the choices that please Him. Hence, your transformation will be hampered if your daily communion with Jesus is shallow. The sincere love and dedication of my parents to Jesus Christ did not only transform them, it left an indelible impact on us, their children.

A New Heart

4. Spiritual Transformation Requires Discipline:

Self-discipline is training yourself to obey rules. You discipline yourself to do what is right in God's sight. Self-discipline activates the power of your will to break negative habits of the flesh. Paul understood that self-discipline had a role in spiritual transformation and the practice of the Christian faith.

> *"But I discipline my body and bring it into subjection, lest, when I have preached to others, I myself should become disqualified" (1 Corinthians 9:27).*

You must discipline yourself to read the Bible daily, pray, fast, or spend long hours in God's presence to be soaked with His power. As a young convert battling with strong opposing desires of the flesh, I was constantly fasting and reading the Bible. I read through the New Testament, Psalms, and Proverbs within two months of my conversion. I fasted at least once a week for personal revival for the last thirty years. This has contributed enormously to my spiritual transformation and growth.

My parents established a strong family altar in our home. I saw Daddy fast and seek God during difficult moments in the family. The answers to his prayers we witnessed helped establish our faith in Christ. Even as a pastor today, I run my family altar as my parents taught me. To encourage me to read God's Word at the family altar, my daddy bought a Bible with a red cover when I was in class seven in primary school. I was the only child in my class who owned a Bible then. What spiritual disciplines are you inculcating in your children for their transformation?

5. Spiritual Transformation is Produced by Suffering:

When properly handled, moments of hardship and suffering can become opportunities for spiritual formation and growth. Deuteronomy 8:2 reveals why God took the children of Israel into the harsh wilderness after He delivered them from Egypt.

> *"And you shall remember that the Lord your God led you all the way these forty years in the wilderness, to humble you and test you, to know what was in your heart, whether you would keep His commandments or not" (Deuteronomy 8:2).*

The wilderness was meant to work transformation in their hearts. Suffering can either make you better or bitter. Some people must suffer pain to become wise. In Psalm 119:67, David describes how suffering delivered him from disobedience and waywardness and gave him an obedient heart.

> *"Before I was afflicted, I went astray, But now I keep Your word."*

Concerning Jesus Christ, Hebrews 5:8 says,

> *"He was a Son, yet He learned obedience by the things which He suffered."*

Do you want to be useful in God's hands? Isaiah 48:10 shows us how He prepares those He would use.

> *"Behold, I have refined you, but not as silver; I have tested you in the furnace of affliction."*

This implies there are certain challenging situations God will not spare you from but will allow you to go through for the transformation of your heart. Don't quickly run away from trials when God is dealing with your heart.

I have learned a lot through hardship:

Today, I appreciate the hardship, lack, rejection, insults, and satanic attacks I encountered during my early days in the faith and ministry. My character and trust in God were polished during those painful moments.

In 1997, I was in the second year of my pastoral ministry in Bafang, Cameroon. Life was tough financially because my monthly support of 25.000 FCFA ($45) was irregular. I had two younger brothers, Edward and Emmanuel, living with me then. One day, we ran out of food and money. We had no dime, no grain of rice, no grain of corn, nor a drop of oil in the house. So, for more than two days, we drank only plain water. Emmanuel and Edward had to trek two kilometers to school every day without eating anything. It had not been long since I ended a fast, and now there was nothing to eat. I ministered during the Bible Study in Church the second evening with much difficulty because I was exhausted from starvation. As the last church member left that evening, I asked God, "So, all these people are blind to the fact we are dying of hunger? Lord, can't you tell one of them to give us food or some money?" They were all blind to our pain. We drank water that evening and slept. You may ask why didn't I tell them we were hungry or go out and borrow food. My next-door neighbor had a shop where I could take food from on credit, but I refused to borrow to survive. Why? I had read in Matthew 6:26 that God who feeds the birds will always provide for me. If birds do not beg or borrow food, why should I do so? This has been my rule of life till today. I don't beg nor borrow food or clothing, no matter what. Early the third morning, a brother from another church knocked on our door and came in with an envelope for me. He said God had sent him to give me the money. We used it to buy food, and our starvation ended. I learned firsthand through the experience that God is a faithful provider for those who love and trust Him. Such difficult moments and my willingness to stand on God's Word shaped my heart to trust and rely on the supernatural supply of my needs. Today, trusting God for big things for my ministry is easy.

A shortcut mentality will short-circuit your destiny. Do everything to build your faith in His faithful promises. Let Him cultivate in you a loyal and persevering heart.

6. *Spiritual Transformation Takes Place as We Obey the Word:*

The practice of God's Word transforms our character and produces maturity. Godly habits are developed as we keep doing what is correct and as we learn the scriptures.

"You will never be able to eat solid spiritual food and understand the deeper things of God's Word until you become better Christians and learn right from wrong BY PRACTICING DOING RIGHT" (Hebrews 5:14 TLB).

You are transformed as you practice doing right. For example, you cultivate a humble heart each time you trample on your pride and apologize for wronging someone instead of justifying yourself. Justifying yourself instead of sincerely repenting hardens your heart. Furthermore, you cultivate spiritual skills as you promptly put into practice God's Word. I mentioned earlier how my mother would quickly sacrifice to apply what she learned during spiritual retreats. You must intentionally graduate from being a hearer to a doer of God's Word (James 1:22-25).

7. *Spiritual Transformation is a Divine Work:*

Our main problem with God is the corruption and crookedness of our hearts. Jeremiah 17:9 describes the deplorable state of man's heart.

"The human heart is the most deceitful of all things, and desperately wicked. Who really knows how bad it is?" (NLT).

The heart always formulates an argument to cover up wickedness or justify disobedience to God's will. Today, some folks trapped in the web of lust and sexual immorality console themselves by saying, "Sin affects the flesh and not the body." By this, they insinuate their sinful actions do not affect their relationship with God. Watch out! Your carnal heart can deceive you into thinking that all is well while you are on your way to hell.

The truth is, you cannot transform your heart by your power; you need divine intervention. Aware of our inability to change our hearts, God assists us. He transforms our hearts through,

- *Divine cleansing:* He cleanses our hearts with the water of the Word as we read, study, meditate, and obey it daily.

  "I will sprinkle clean water on you, and you will be clean; I will cleanse you from all your impurities and from all your idols" (Ezekiel 36:25).

- *Divine heart transplant:* God supernaturally replaces our wicked hearts with godly hearts.

  "I will give you a new heart and put a new spirit in you; I will remove from you your heart of stone and give you a heart of flesh" (Ezekiel 36:26).

- *Divine circumcision:* Through supernatural circumcision, God cuts off the foreskin of our flesh to release our will that has been imprisoned. An uncircumcised heart always resists the Holy Spirit (Acts 7:51).

  "...TRUE CIRCUMCISION is not merely obeying the letter of the law; rather, it IS A CHANGE OF HEART produced by the Spirit. And a person with a changed heart seeks praise from God, not from people" (Romans 2:29 NLT).

- *Divine purification by fire:* There is a dimension of the transformation of our hearts that requires the fire of the Holy Spirit.

  "For he is like a refiner's fire and like fullers' soap. He will sit as a refiner and purifier of silver. He will purify the sons of Levi and refine them like gold and silver, and they will bring offerings in righteousness to the LORD" (Malachi 3:2-3).

Refiners use scorching fire to burn out the dross and obtain pure gold and silver. Similarly, the Holy Spirit exposes and purges deep-rooted sinful dispositions in our nature with fire. According to John the Baptist, the baptism of the Holy Spirit is not about noise; it is an encounter with purifying fire for liberation from the web of iniquity.

"He who is coming after me [Jesus Christ] is mightier than I...He will baptize you with the Holy Spirit and fire... but the chaff he will burn with unquenchable fire" (Matthew 3:11).

We must emphasize to believers the fundamental purpose of the baptism of the Holy Spirit, which is fire for purification from the chaffs of sin and empowerment to live for Jesus Christ. As crucial as it is, the quest for power for signs and wonders must never outride the passion for being empowered by the Holy Spirit to live like Christ. In Matthew 7:21-22, Jesus warned that on judgment day, He would cast away some workers of miracles who were also workers of iniquity.

- *Impartation of divine life:* Knowing how limited our will is, God has made provisions to strengthen us from the inside to do His will by filling us with His Holy Spirit.

  "And I will put my Spirit in you and move you to follow my decrees and be careful to keep my laws" (Ezekiel 36:27).

Are you hungry for a new heart – a heart that loves and submits to God's will? Cry out to God for help. He will do deep work for the renewal and restoration of your heart.

Draw Power Continuously From the Cross

As a believer who desires to experience spiritual transformation and growth, you must understand how to draw power from the cross. The cross of Jesus Christ is the source of our power for transformation and living a victorious life. Jesus Christ defeated sin, Satan, the world, and sickness on the cross and gave us victory.

Through divine revelation, Paul declares in Galatians 2:20,

> *"I am crucified with Christ; it is no longer I who live, but Christ lives in me..."*

What does it mean to be crucified with Christ? It means our old man (Sinful nature) has been crucified with Christ. When Christ went to the cross, we were in Him, so we died with Him when He died. You must continuously apply this truth to draw the power of resurrection for a victorious life.

1. **Believe and confess that you have been crucified with Christ:**

Paul believed it. You too should believe it to be free. Now that you have been crucified with Christ take note of this truth,

> *"And those who are Christ's have crucified the flesh with its passions and desires" (Galatians 5:24).*

By faith, keep sin where it belongs; crucified/dead with our old man. Sin is dead.

2. **Believe and confess that you are a brand-new creature in Christ:**

Believe this truth! You died with Christ; when He rose from the dead, you rose with Him. You are now a new creature, completely different from who you used to be. It is not about how you feel. In Christ, God has justified you (Romans 5:1). You are no longer under condemnation (Romans 8:1). Heaven sees you as a recreated entity. Stop relying on your feelings and past; you are a new creation.

3. **Keep reminding yourself that you are dead with Christ:**

According to Romans 6:11, you have to

> *"RECKON YOURSELF TO BE DEAD INDEED TO SIN, but alive in Christ Jesus our Lord."*

A regenerated believer is "Dead indeed to sin." You have to know this and declare it continuously. I have realized that whenever I say to myself, "I have been crucified with Christ. I am a dead man." Desires of the flesh just evaporate. A dead man cannot steal or fornicate—puncture temptation with this truth.

4. Do not tolerate sin in your life:
In Romans 6:12-13, Paul emphasizes,

> *"...DO NOT LET SIN REIGN in your mortal body, that you should obey it in its lusts. Do not present your members to sin as instruments for unrighteousness, but present yourselves to God."*

Do not permit your old man/sinful nature to resurrect by yielding to its temptations. Deliberately avoid situations where you can easily be trapped in sin. To maintain a clean heart, draw boundaries in your life: (1) Intentionally stay away from the wrong people (2 Corinthians 6:14). (2) Preserve your ears and eyes from profane music and pictures (Job 31:1). (3) Let those around you know you belong to Jesus Christ and are different (Matthew 10:32-33). (4) Make up your mind to please Jesus Christ at all costs (1 Peter 4:1-2).

In summary
God is recruiting men and women willing to be purged, empowered, and deployed **for** revival this season. You have this book in your hands by divine arrangement. God is calling you for something greater than you have ever imagined. Can you yield yourself to Him and allow the Holy Spirit to do a deep work of transformation in you? There are many available vessels, but few are usable for God's work of revival. You decide today to be available and allow God to make you usable.

Go before God now with an open heart and sincerely ask the Holy Spirit to reveal the deep issues of your heart that must be dealt with. Repent before Him and collaborate with the Holy Spirit prayerfully to deal with them. Do open confession and restitution where necessary. Just allow the Holy Spirit to have His way in your life; your heart will change.

PRAYER POINTS
1. *Father, thank You for the privilege to be part of this great revival and prophetic program, in Jesus' name.*
2. *Father, thank You for revival and restoration in my life this season, in Jesus' name.*

3. Father, thank You for what You will do in the lives of all the believers fasting and praying with this book, in Jesus' name.
4. Father, thank You for the gift of Your Word as an instrument for my transformation, in Jesus' name.
5. Father, I worship You for choosing me to be an agent of revival this season, in Jesus' name.
6. Place your hand on your head and pray 5 times, "I welcome the fire, the light, and the river of the Holy Spirit in my life, in Jesus' name."
7. Pray in tongues for at least 10 minutes if you can.
8. Father, open my spiritual eyes to see myself the way You see me, in Jesus' name.
9. Father, expose deep things in my life for total transformation, in Jesus' name.
10. Place your hand on your head and pray 5 times, "You veil of spiritual blindness over my mind, catch fire now, in Jesus' name."
11. You veil of spiritual blindness over the mind of my husband, wife, children, etc., burn to ashes, in Jesus' name.
12. O Merciful Father, arise and open a mighty door of salvation in my family, in Jesus' name.
13. Pray for people you desire to be saved.
14. Father, You have promised to take away my stony heart; remove every stone from my heart, in Jesus' name.
15. O Father, open the fountain of the blood of Jesus and purge my heart of every root of iniquity, in Jesus' name.
16. Father, let Your living waters flow over my soul for profound cleansing, in Jesus' name.
17. Place your hand on your heart and pray 7 times, "Fire of God, fall now and purify my spiritual foundation, in Jesus' name."
18. Father, restore a new heart in me that loves Your Word and Your ways, in Jesus' name.
19. Place your hand on your head and pray 5 times, "I reject every satanic seed planted in my mind, in Jesus' name."
20. Holy Ghost fire, fall now and set my mind completely free, in Jesus' name.
21. I receive the mind of Christ, in Jesus' name.
22. O Lord Jesus Christ, I surrender my will and desires to You; establish Your rule over all the areas of my life from today.
23. Lord Jesus, I accept Your will for my life even when it doesn't excite my flesh, in Jesus' name.

24. *I lose my soul from every entanglement with the wrong people in my life, in Jesus' name.*
25. *I break every chain of ungodly soul ties over my life, in Jesus' name.*
26. *I lose my children from the bondage of evil manipulations of ungodly friends, in Jesus' name.*
27. *Place your hand on your head and pray 7 times, "Holy Spirit, fill me to the overflow, in Jesus' name."*
28. *I receive the power to know and do God's will in my life, in Jesus' name.*
29. *I receive the power to obey God even when it is difficult, in Jesus' name.*
30. *I receive the power to enjoy the new life in Christ, in Jesus' name.*
31. *I believe in Jesus Christ and have received Him in my heart; I activate the power to function as a Son in Christ.*
32. *Father, let the power of God incubate me until Christ is fully formed in my heart, in Jesus' name.*
33. *Father, thank You because You paid the full price for my total freedom from sin, Satan, and curses on the cross.*
34. *By the finished work of the cross, I declare my total victory over sin, Satan, and all forms of oppression in the mighty name of Jesus.*
35. *Father, thank You for revealing that the cross is the instrument of my victory over Satan, sin, and sicknesses.*
36. *Father, I believe I died with Christ, and my flesh was crucified. Sin shall no longer rule me because the man of sin in me is crucified.*
37. *Father, open my eyes to see deeper into the mystery of the crucified life in Christ.*
38. *Father, let the power of the cross begin to work in all the members of my body, spirit, and soul, in Jesus' name.*
39. *Father, use me to draw the lost to Your Kingdom in Jesus' name.*
40. *Father, fill me with Your light and help me to dominate spiritual darkness in my place of work.*
41. *Father, give me the grace to follow, copy, and emulate those You have placed before me.*
42. *O Lord Jesus Christ, increase in my life as I decrease, in Jesus' Name.*
43. *O Father, pour out Your Spirit of revival and restore hunger for the truth in our hearts.*
44. *Father, pour out the Spirit of revival and restore a passion for Jesus Christ in our hearts.*
45. *Father, pour out the Spirit of revival and restore the fear of God in our families.*
46. *Father, pour out the Spirit of revival and bring back backsliders to the Kingdom.*

47. *Father, arise and release Your fire afresh on the Church this season, in Jesus' name.*
48. *Place your hand on your chest and pray, "Holy Spirit, take over my thoughts and begin to influence all my actions, in Jesus' name."*
49. *I receive special grace to be a soul-winner from today, in Jesus' name.*
50. *Thank You for giving me a new heart, in Jesus' name.*

Chapter 2
Days 4-6

A Heart Hungry for God

"Blessed are those who hunger and thirst for righteousness, for they shall be filled" (Matthew 5:6).

William J. Seymour (1870–1922) had the type of heart God needed for an agent of revival. His heart was desperately hungry for God. He became God's chosen vessel who spearheaded the Azusa Street Revival, which gave birth to the modern Pentecostal movement. He was born in Centerville, Louisiana, the eldest son of freed slaves. He grew up in extreme poverty and spent much of his early years traveling throughout the United States to obtain work. While in Ohio, he had severe smallpox, which scarred his face and left him blind in one eye.

Seymour, who had recently joined the Holiness movement, began to seek God passionately. In the early 1900s, many were asking God for a Pentecostal outpouring of holiness and power for signs and wonders. In 1905, the thirty-six-year-old Seymour, anxiously hungry for God, went to Houston, Texas, to meet Charles Parham, who operated a bible school. He had heard that people were experiencing the baptism of the Holy Spirit accompanied by speaking with other tongues and other supernatural manifestations through Parham's ministry.

Nothing Could Stop Him

Because of the segregation laws of the time, Seymour could not officially attend Parham's Bible School with the whites. Still, his hunger for God compelled him to sit often in the corridor outside the classroom door to listen to the lectures. He later testified;

> "Before I met Parham, such a hunger to have more of God was in my heart that I prayed for five hours a day for two and a half years. I got to Los Angeles, and there, the hunger was not less but more. I prayed, 'God, what can I do?' The Spirit said, 'Pray more.' 'But Lord, I am praying five hours a day now.' I increased my hours of prayer to seven and prayed for a year and a half more. I prayed to God to give what Parham preached, the real Holy Ghost and fire with tongues, love, and power of God like the apostles had."

In early 1906, Seymour was invited to become the pastor of a small holiness church in Los Angeles, CA. His arrival in Los Angeles stirred the holiness community there because of his bold preaching about the baptism of the Holy Spirit and speaking in tongues. His ministry was rejected by the prominent lay leader who founded the church because of his enthusiastic Pentecostal emphasis. Only a week after his arrival, they padlocked the church door against him after his first sermon on Acts 2:4. Seymour was left without a church to preach in.

Refusing to submit to fear and discouragement, he formed a predominantly Black home prayer group at Richard Asberry's home on Bonnie Bray Street, which met regularly. Seymour pressed on in faith with a firm conviction that the blessing was on its way, even though he still needed to be baptized by the Holy Spirit with the biblical evidence of speaking with tongues or any of his hearers.

On April 9, 1906, on the third day of a ten-day fast, Seymour and the others received what they had been seeking: more of God – infilling of the Holy Spirit, speaking in tongues *'glossolalia,'* and other charismatic manifestations of God's power. This was the beginning of the Azusa Street Revival, which impacted the world for more than 100 years.

God's Power at Work

God continued to pour out rivers of living water and baptized His people with fresh fire for over three years. Thousands were saved,

healed, and baptized in the Holy Spirit. News about the revival spread like wildfire. "Day after day, the meetings continued, almost without interruption. Sometimes there were as many as nine per day. Services often lasted from early in the morning until late at night. The building was always open, and the meetings started without a leader initiating them."[5]
According to Robert Owens,

> "For weeks, the meetings would blend into one another and last twenty-four hours a day. The building was always open, and the meetings started without a leader initiating them… The power of God would flow through the room at different times, knocking people down… Often masses of people would simultaneously rush to the altar to seek after God."[6]

Frank Bartleman, an eyewitness of the Azusa Street Revival, wrote,

> "Seeking souls could be found under the power almost any hour, night, and day. The place was never closed or empty. The people came to meet God. He was always there… Speaking in tongues was often manifested, followed by interpretations… A dozen might be on their feet at one time, trembling under the power of God."[7]

Owens writes,

"Many testified about being drawn to the revival by the Holy Spirit. Some testified of having visions or dreams directing them to Azusa…Two favorite hymns of the revival were, *The Comforter Has Come* and *Under the Blood*."[8]

Amazing Scenes at Azusa

- Scores of personal and eyewitness accounts attest that many who came to ridicule the meetings were knocked to the floor, where they seemed to wrestle with unseen opponents, sometimes for hours. These people generally arose convicted of sin and seeking God.

- Scores of people were seen dropping into a prostrate position in the streets before they ever reached the church. Then many would get up, speaking in tongues without any influence from the Azusa people. God had come to accomplish His work!

- Divine love was wonderfully manifest in the meetings. They would not even allow an unkind word to be said against their opposers or the churches.

- Many healings took place during the Azusa Street Revival. A typical example is the story of a young girl who attended the service one evening and was baptized in the Holy Spirit. The following day, she went to the meeting and saw a woman who had been crippled for thirty-two years. Prompted by the Holy Spirit, the girl approached the woman and said, "Jesus wants to heal you." Hearing these words, the woman's toes and feet straightened out, and she began to walk.

- During the meeting, a young woman testified that God had baptized her with the Holy Spirit when she suddenly broke into tongues. After the meeting, the reporter sought her out and asked her where she had learned the language of his native country. She answered that she didn't know what she had said and spoke only English. He then told her that she had given an entirely accurate account of his sinful life, all in the language of his native tongue.

- Other eyewitnesses reported seeing a holy glow emanating from the building that could be seen from streets away.

- Others reported hearing sounds from the wooden building like explosions reverberating around the neighborhood. Such phenomena caused onlookers to call the Fire Department several times when a blaze or explosion was reported at the church building.

- One man at Azusa said, "I would have rather lived six months at that time than fifty years of ordinary life. I have stopped more than once within two blocks of the place and prayed for strength before I dared go on. The presence of the Lord was so real."

- Some reporters who came to investigate the revival were baptized in the lodgings.

Walls of Racism Broken
Like a mighty flood, the revival swept away the walls of racism. At a time when racial segregation was common, the blending of races in the meetings was tangible. African-Americans, Asians, Europeans, Hispanics, and whites drawn by the Holy Spirit prayed, sang, and sought God's touch together. Frank Bartleman wrote, "The blood washed away the color line."[9] Denzil Miller added, "The line between clergy and laity was blurred. Active participation in the meetings was opened to all."[10]

Seymour's preaching was simple and direct and covered themes like salvation by a personal acceptance of Jesus as Savior, sanctification by renunciation of sin and turning from worldliness, abandonment of rigid traditions and the legalisms of man-made religion, the baptism of the Holy Spirit with speaking in tongues, divine healing, and the premillennial return of Jesus.

The Revival Impacted World Missions
The Azusa Revival contributed immensely to revamping world missions. Denzil Miller identifies three distinct ways through which this happened: First, several individuals, after receiving Spirit baptism at Azusa, went out immediately to preach the Gospel as missionaries to home and foreign fields. Secondly, missionaries from different fields worldwide who heard about the revival went there received God's fire for the work through the baptism of the Holy Spirit. Finally, new missionary movements were born after church leaders visited Azusa and were baptized in the Holy Spirit.[11]

Within nine months, many missionaries were already being sent throughout the West Coast of the United States, and thirteen missionaries departed to Africa. Just two years after the outpouring of the Holy Spirit in 1906, missionaries commissioned in the Azusa Street Mission could be found in Mexico, Canada, Western Europe, the Middle East, West Africa, and several countries in Asia…South Africa, Central, and Eastern Europe, and even Northern Russia.[12]

Jennie Evans Moore Seymour: A Woman Mightily Used of God
Jennie Seymour, wife of William Seymour, has been called perhaps, "The most influential woman in the life and ministry of William Joseph Seymour".[13] She was one of seven people who received the Spirit and

began to speak in tongues during the initial outpouring on Bonnie Brae Street. With her speaking in tongues, however, came another miracle. Robert Owens writes, "She began to play beautiful music on an old upright piano and to sing in what people said was Hebrew. Until this time, she had never played the piano, and although she never took a lesson, she could play the instrument for the rest of her life."[14]

Seymour, an Instrument in God's Hands

Bartleman, his co-laborer and fellow leader at the Azusa Street Mission, described Seymour by saying, "He was very plain, spiritual, and humble… Brother Seymour generally sat behind two empty shoe boxes, one on top of the other. He usually kept his head inside the top one during the meeting in prayer. There was no pride there."[15]

William H. Durham was a pastor from Chicago who traveled to Azusa Street. His description of Seymour was this: "He walks and talks with God. His power is in his weakness. He seems to maintain a helpless dependence on God and is as simple-hearted as a little child, and at the same time is so filled with God that you feel the love and power every time you get near him."[16]

William Seymour was a man who fully surrendered to God, and the Lord used him mightily to bring about a major reawakening to early 20th-century America and, eventually, the whole world.

William Seymour died before he could accomplish many of his goals. He had planned to establish schools and rescue missions and form other congregations, but these dreams were never fulfilled. Still, despite the rapid decline in his influence, Seymour had a tremendous impact on the Pentecostal movement, which has grown to include about one billion believers throughout the world.

The Urgent Need for Hungry Men and Women

William Seymour's story testifies that revival fire burns in every generation through the lives of consecrated men and women who are hungry for more of God. In fact, the difference between a generation that experiences revival and that which does not is the presence or absence of hungry men and women. Today, all those doing outstanding exploits in God's Kingdom are hungry and thirsty men and women. They are driven by passion and vision to know God and fulfill their divine destinies.

What is Hunger for God?

Merriam's English Dictionary defines "Hunger" as "Having a strong craving for food." Generally, hunger is not just about physical food; humans also crave emotional, intellectual, and spiritual nourishment. Just as desire in your body drives you to eat physical food, the hunger of your spirit and soul propels you to feed on spiritual food – God's Word and worship.

"Hunger for God" is the fervent desire in your heart to know Him and have Him meet your deepest needs that money and material things cannot provide. It is seeking the living waters of the Holy Spirit to quench the thirst of your soul. Above all, it is a passion to become all God wants you to be in Christ. An author said, "If you are not hungry for God, you are probably full of yourself." How profound is your hunger for God? Today, many who are full of themselves call God-seekers, fanatics. If you were to see the awful state of your spiritual nakedness and vulnerability, you would pursue God like a treasure hunter does.

An unquenchable hunger for God is the most valuable spiritual asset you can possess. Let nothing kill your hunger for spiritual things. Losing your appetite for God indicates you are spiritually sick and on the path to death. Furthermore, to lose consciousness of your urgent need for God is a sign of spiritual death. There are several spiritually sick and dead people in the church.

Marks of a Hungry Heart

A heart that is sincerely hungry for God is focused on being with Jesus Christ, becoming like Him, and pleasing Him. Spiritually hungry people emerge as true Disciples of Christ.

1. A Hungry Heart Pursues God's Presence

A man or woman hungry for God always wants to be in His presence. In Psalm 27:4, David expresses his intense hunger for God's presence.

> *"The one thing I want from God, the thing I seek most of all, is the privilege of meditating in his Temple, LIVING IN HIS PRESENCE EVERY DAY OF MY LIFE, delighting in his incomparable perfections and glory" (TLB).*

In the Gospel of John 12:26, Jesus underlines that a passion for abiding in His presence is a mark of a true servant of God.

> *"Anyone who wants to serve me must follow me because my servants must be where I am. And the Father will honor anyone who serves me" (NLT).*

Hence, your claim to be God's servant is unfounded if you don't practice His presence.

If we are going to become agents of revival, there is an urgent call to answer – spending time with God. We must all realize that being with Jesus Christ is far more critical than getting busy for Him. Your ministry will not impact lives until you stay with Him and become pregnant with His life and power. Time well spent with God is never wasted. William Seymour became a tremendous channel of revival because he invested hours upon hours basking in God's glory. You cannot give out what you have not received. How much time do you invest in seeking God for instruction, direction, and impartation to accomplish your Kingdom assignment? To rush out there for ministry without receiving a tangible deposit from the Holy Spirit is to waste the greatest opportunity of your life. Let us return to God's presence for equipment!

2. A Hungry Heart Pursues God's Knowledge

One who is hungry for God pursues Jesus Christ; to know and please Him. In several verses of Psalm 119, David expresses his passion for knowing and keeping God's statutes, laws, commandments, and precepts.

> *"O LORD; teach me your statutes" (vs. 12). "I shall keep Your law; Indeed, I shall observe it with my whole heart" (vs. 15). "Teach me good judgment and knowledge" (vs. 66). "I cry out with my whole heart; Hear me, O LORD!" (vs. 145)*

David excelled in Israel as a king, military general, priest, prophet, musician, songwriter, and psalmist because he was a lover of God's presence and knowledge.

In Matthew 11:28-29, Jesus Christ announced to His potential disciples,

> *"Come to me, all of you who are weary and carry heavy burdens, and I will give you rest. Take my yoke upon you. LET ME TEACH YOU, because I am humble and gentle at heart, and you will find rest for your souls" (NLT).*

Agents of revival are seekers who want to know God's ways. They want to learn from Jesus Christ how to lead their lives and ministry. Sometimes I am shocked by what I see people doing in the name of ministry. I wonder whether Jesus Christ would endorse such craftiness and abuse of church members if He were physically present.

You can never be a good teacher of the Gospel if you have not been well taught. You can only lead effectively once you have learned to follow. Jesus Christ uses men to teach us His ways. Hence, you must be willing to submit and learn under tutors and mentors. Those trying to teach others without thorough learning constitute a terrible cankerworm that has plagued the modern Church. Don't be part of them. They will not last. Let Jesus teach you first before you start teaching others. You cannot teach others to do what you have not learned to do.

God's prophetic word for this season is,

"For the earth will be filled with the knowledge of the glory of the LORD as the waters cover the sea" (Habakkuk 2:14 ESV).

May you become one among those through whom this prophecy will be fulfilled in your family, church, community, and nation in Jesus' name.

3. A Hungry Heart Pursues God in Prayer

Every spiritual revival is preceded by a season of fervent prayer. Such Christ-centered prayers rise from the bosoms of men and women passionate about manifesting God's kingdom among men. Before the revival on Pentecost Day, the disciples were in God's presence, fasting and praying for ten days (Acts 1). Also, we remark that every move of God recorded in the book of Acts resulted from His people's fervent prayer. God's modus operandi has not shifted. Effective prayer is the key to spiritual revival. We mentioned earlier how William Seymour gave himself hours of prayer daily for almost ten years to provoke the great Pentecostal revival at Azusa.

The death of the prayer altar of a family or church is the beginning of spiritual death. Sadly, these days, prayer meetings are becoming scantier in most churches. Dear child of God, what are you counting on when you fail to pray? Maybe you blame your weak prayer life on your busy schedule. Watch out! Are you busier than Daniel, the Prime Minister of Babylon? He prayed three times daily despite his tight schedule (Daniel

6:10). He knew the risk of working without prayer. As a result of this, he rose to prominence among sorcerers, magicians, and occultists. The role Jesus attributed to prayer in His life indicates we cannot survive without it.

In Acts 6:4, the Apostles noticed that the revival fire in the church was dying out because of distraction, so they boldly declared,

"We will devote ourselves to prayer and to the ministry of the word" (ESV).

Is it not time for ministers of the Gospel to make a similar resolution? How long shall we continue struggling to do God's work without Him? Prayer is vital in bringing God into any Kingdom venture. A lot is going wrong in your family, church, community, and nation. God wants you to arise and pray until heaven intervenes. Leonard Ravenhill said, "A minister who is not praying is playing. A church that is not praying is straying." Are you praying, playing, or straying?

4. A Hungry Heart Pursues God's Power

We cannot create an impact in God's Kingdom without power. The anointing – the power of the Holy Spirit is the secret for manifesting a colorful destiny. Jesus Christ enjoyed a glorious ministry. Acts 10:38 points out that the anointing was His secret.

"How God anointed Jesus of Nazareth with the Holy Spirit and with power. He went about doing good and healing all who were oppressed by the devil, for God was with him" (ESV).

In Luke 24:49, Jesus emphasized that His disciples should wait and receive His power before engaging in evangelism and missions.

"And now I will send the Holy Spirit upon you, just as my Father promised. Don't begin telling others yet—stay here in the city until the Holy Spirit comes and fills you with power from heaven" (NLT).

They received the power and went out to shake their world for Jesus.

Satanic powers are causing havoc all over the place. Shall we fold our hands and continue to preach a powerless Gospel that cannot chase away a fly? Through this message, God is stirring your heart to seek His power to become a genuine witness. You must arise in the power of the

Holy Spirit and stop the mockery that is going on around you against Jesus Christ.

In James 5:16, Apostle James, a mighty man of prayer, shows us that effective prayer is the key to divine power.

> *"The earnest prayer of a righteous man has great power and wonderful results" (James 5:16 TLB).*

There is no release of power without prayer. Powerless Christianity is the fruit of prayerlessness. Jesus Christ spent forty days in the wilderness and returned with great power (Luke 4:14).

It is time to seek God for the release of His power in our lives. Refuse to be a powerless Christian tossed around by every evil spirit.

5. **A Hungry Heart Pursues God's Purpose and Glory**

Agents of revival move God because they pursue His purpose and glory. Your primary responsibility as a believer is to find God's will, purpose, and plan for your life and commit yourself to accomplishing it. Hebrews 10:7, talking about Jesus' earthly mission, says,

> *"Behold, I HAVE COME TO DO YOUR WILL, O God, as it is written of me in the scroll of the book" (ESV).*

Jesus clearly understood that God's will for Him was death on the cross for the redemption of humanity. He fully embraced His destiny without wavering, even though it was a bitter pill. Throughout His ministry, He prayed fervently to know and do His Father's will.

> *"I seek not my own will but the will of him who sent me" (John 5:30).*

In John 17:4, he prayed,

> *"I glorified you on earth, having accomplished the work that you gave me to do" (ESV).*

God the Father backed every step He took because He existed on earth to fulfill heaven's agenda.

Have you found out God's will, purpose, or plan for your life? Are you pursuing it? If we will move God's hand in this season, our focus must be to give ourselves entirely to His will, purpose, and plan for our lives. Do not run your life by imitation; go by divine revelation. God will not open the floodgates of heaven to pour blessings on a project He did not design for you. Hence, ensure you are at your duty post. Don't copy another man's calling; you will not be rewarded. Look for your place and fit into God's mission. You are not wasting if you spent all your life serving faithfully under the leadership of someone with a genuine Apostolic mantle or serving in a mission. You must not start your own church or ministry like others. Only do it if God has sent you.

Likewise, let us stop all this usurping of God's glory and begin to project Jesus Christ as Lord over all we have and do. Like John the Baptizer, let your motto become,

"He must increase, but I must decrease" (John 3:30).

Let people see Jesus Christ more, Hear Him, and feel Him more in your ministry. Refuse to let people amplify your name above His name. Constantly remind the people celebrating you that the church, ministry, anointing, gifts, and blessings you are experiencing belong to Jesus; you are His servant. Give Him all the glory; your life will never lack His glory and power.

Where are Hungry Men and Women?

Where are the hungry men and women in the Kingdom who would stir God's revival fire in the hearts of people of this generation? God is looking for human instruments to break the yoke of spiritual apathy, moral bankruptcy, religiosity, compromise, worldliness, sensuality, and rebellion from the souls of His people. Will you answer the call today to become an agent of revival? God will baptize you with holy hunger for His glory.

In fulfillment of Acts 2:17-19, we trust God to raise mighty revivalists in the nations like William Seymour and the others for revival and restoration in the nations.

"And in the last days, it shall be, God declares, that I will pour out my Spirit on all flesh, and your sons and your daughters shall prophesy, and your young men shall see visions, and your old men shall dream dreams..."

May you become a mighty instrument in God's hand, in Jesus' name.

PRAYER POINTS

1. *Father, thank You for the work of transformation taking place in my heart, in Jesus' name.*
2. *Father, thank You for the wind of revival blowing in the land, in Jesus' name.*
3. *Father, thank You because the undefiled who walk in Your ways are truly blessed.*

4. *Father, I praise Your name because those who seek You will find You.*
5. *Father, thank You because I will see Your glory in this season, in Jesus's name.*
6. *Father, I praise You because my blessings are guaranteed as I seek You with my whole heart, in Jesus' name.*
7. *Father, thank You for choosing me to be Your treasured possession, in Jesus' name.*
8. *Father, thank You because all Your thoughts and plans towards me are glorious.*
9. *Father, thank You for this day and for providing a way in Christ Jesus for my total deliverance.*
10. *Place your hand on your chest and pray 7 times, "Blood of Jesus, cleanse me from any evil that gives Satan the ground to accuse me, in Jesus' name."*
11. *I am a child of God, and the blood of Jesus cancels every claim of Satan and his host over my life.*
12. *Lay your hand over your heart and pray 5 times, "I root out every evil seed that fights God's Word in my heart, in Jesus' name."*
13. *I break the yoke of spiritual barrenness, in Jesus' name.*
14. *I cast out the spirit of distraction from my life, in Jesus' name.*
15. *I break the yoke of shallow Christianity from my life, in Jesus' name.*
16. *I cast out every spirit of spiritual blindness from my life, in Jesus' name.*
17. *Holy ghost fire, consume every evil foundation resisting my consecration, in Jesus' name.*
18. *I command the yoke of human tradition over my soul to break now, in Jesus' name.*
19. *I break the power of confusion in my life, in Jesus' name.*
20. *Place your hand on your heart and pray 7 times, "Fire of God fall now and consume every wicked appetite in me that resists holiness, in Jesus' name."*
21. *I bind and cast out every demonic spirit assigned to waste my spiritual life, in Jesus' name.*
22. *Raise your two hands and pray 7 times, "I receive a garment of fire now, in Jesus' name."*
23. *Let the anointing of the Holy Spirit soak me from my head to my feet now, in Jesus' name.*
24. *Father, restore my body, soul, and spirit fully, now, in Jesus' name.*
25. *Father, baptize my heart with a deep hunger for Your presence and power, in Jesus' name.*
26. *Fire of God, fall on us now and restore a deep hunger for God's Word, in Jesus' name.*

27. *I receive fresh oil on my ears to hear God's voice better, in Jesus' name.*
28. *I receive divine light into my eyes to see glorious things in God's Word, in Jesus' name.*
29. *You power of darkness waging war against my prayer altar, be arrested by fire and cast away, in Jesus' name.*
30. *You evil altar, speaking against my prayer life, that of my family and the Church, catch fire, now! In Jesus' name.*
31. *O Lord, arise and restore the fire of fasting and prayer in the Church in this land, in Jesus' name.*
32. *O Lord, give me the grace to keep Your commandments diligently, in Jesus' name.*
33. *Father, as I seek God and keep Your Word, let shame be far from me, in Jesus' name.*
34. *Father, let Your Word prosper abundantly in my life, family, and Church, in Jesus' name.*
35. *Father, arise and restore miracles, signs, and wonders in the Church.*
36. *Father, pour out Your Spirit and cause the ministers of the Gospel to be seekers of God.*
37. *Father, pour out Your Spirit and restore hunger for Jesus Christ in the hearts of the people of this nation.*
38. *Dear Holy Spirit, shine Your light in this land and reveal Christ to those hungry for the truth, in Jesus' name.*
39. *Father, arise and deliver the Church from falsehood and ungodliness, in Jesus' name.*
40. *Father, pour out Your Spirit in the Church and raise mighty agents of revival in Jesus' name.*
41. *Father, pour out Your Spirit afresh in the Church for a massive revival, in Jesus' name.*
42. *Father, pour out Your Spirit afresh and rescue us from empty religion without power, in Jesus' name.*
43. *Father, release Your power and strengthen us to continue in prayer until we see Your glory in our families, churches, and nations, in Jesus' name.*
44. *Fire of God, fall and purge our pulpits of human philosophies and heresies, in Jesus' name.*
45. *Father, rend the heavens and send us the rain of increase, in Jesus' name.*
46. *O Lord, pour out Your Spirit afresh and fill us with a deep hatred for sin, in Jesus' name.*

47. *Father, take hold of Your children and begin to use them to influence change in this nation, in Jesus' name.*
48. *Father, open the floodgates of heaven and visit us in this season, in Jesus' name.*
49. *Father, have mercy on this nation and turn to us for healing.*
50. *Father, cause those leading churches to catch a fresh vision of the role of prayer in the expansion of God's Kingdom.*
51. *Father, release Your Spirit abundantly for the emergence of men and women who will run with the fire of revival in this land.*
52. *Father, release Your Spirit mightily for the rise of anointed praise and worship leaders to lead the Church into revival.*

Chapter 3
Days 7-9

A Broken Heart

"The LORD is near to those who have a broken heart, And saves such as have a contrite spirit" (Psalm 34:18).

One who would accommodate the Holy Spirit and be used as God desires needs a broken heart. An unrepentant, proud, rebellious, unforgiving, bitter, malicious, and wicked heart renders us unusable even if we are available. I discovered with time that God had blessed me with a special treasure; a wife with a broken heart.

Saturday 9 October 1999, was our wedding day in Bamenda, Cameroon. Two days later, I moved with my wife, Anna Nama, to our station, Bafang, in the West Region of Cameroon. Within a few weeks, I discovered that my wife was a woman of few words with a broken heart. She would say one word and switch to the quiet mode during the next quarter of an hour when we sat to discuss our differences. Her quietness was not a way to despise me, but the virtue of self-control knitted into her phlegmatic temperament. But this wasn't very comfortable for me because, by nature, I like to express myself with many words. Sometimes, I wanted her to talk more or debate with me, but she would sit quietly and stare at me. I understood with time that God, in His infinite mercy and wisdom, had given me the right partner I needed. Marriage experts believe couples that complement each other temperament-wise make healthy marriages. For example, two extroverted people may not form a good pair. Contrariwise, introverts, and extroverts have a greater chance of making a great married couple. In my case, I needed someone with the quality of temperament Anna had to stabilize me. Thank God for giving me just the best.

She Always Says, "I am sorry."

Within a short time together in marriage, the broken nature of Anna's heart began to show up whenever we had a misunderstanding. With an angelic softness, she would promptly say, "I'm sorry." Sometimes, she would apologize even when she was not at fault. Often when I was on my nerves and began to raise my voice, expecting that she would engage me in an argument, she said, "Excuse me, I am sorry," and shut up. If I continued talking, she would release another "I am sorry." Occasionally, I would talk alone for some time and shut off because she would not answer me back. I was astonished that she could say, "I am sorry," several times daily. Initially, I told myself, "Maybe this woman is trying to manipulate me." But with time, I got a strong witness in my spirit that it was not an escapist strategy. She was pouring out what was in her heart – brokenness, humility, and simplicity.

My wife has continuously used the phrase "I am sorry" as a potent and efficient fire extinguisher in our marriage during our last twenty-four years together. The result is that no misunderstanding led to a quarrel, not to talk of a fight. Lynn Johnston says, "An apology is the superglue of life. It can repair just about anything." I agree with him because "I am sorry" has continuously revived, restored, and preserved our marriage.

I Learned to Say it Too

The vital lesson I have learned from my wife, Anna, all these years is to stop talking whenever she says, "I'm sorry." Two years ago, while discussing how "I am sorry" had contributed to building and preserving our marriage all these years, she reminded me that sometimes I continue to talk when she says, "I am sorry." I laughed and told her that when water is poured on fire, it doesn't go out instantly. There is usually much smoke before the fire dies out. I was trying to let her know that I am still in the school of apology after twenty-two years of marriage. It is a good school. You can join me.

Today, I can easily say "I'm sorry" when she is offended, unlike during the first ten years of our marriage. In the past, I either remained dumb or would raise my manly voice to justify myself. I sincerely appreciate God for using my wife to do an excellent transformation work in my heart. I still trust Him for a more profound work in my heart to become more like Jesus Christ, my Lord.

What is a Broken Heart?

Webster's Revised Unabridged Dictionary defines "A broken heart" as "Having the spirits depressed or crushed by grief or despair." The Chambers 20th Century Dictionary defines "Brokenness" as "Bankrupt, fragmentary or humbled." Hence, one with a broken heart expresses profound humility, meekness, submission, compassion, and simplicity.

Anna Wishart, in an article, *"The Meaning of Brokenness in the Bible,"* presents three meanings of brokenness, which I think will help us better understand the concept:

1) ***Broken because of our condition:*** This is a repentant spirit resulting from realizing our sinfulness. David became remorseful after his illicit affair with Bathsheba (Psalm 51). Peter also experienced brokenness after denying Jesus Christ (Mark 14:66-72).

2) ***Broken by the world around us:*** The hardship, suffering, pain, wars, and crisis you experience in your family and society can break your heart. In Lamentations 3, Prophet Jeremiah is grieving over the suffering and loss in Israel. Jesus died on the cross with a broken heart because He bore the burden of the sins of the world (Isaiah 53:3-5). My heart is broken whenever I watch TV news and see the evil in our society.[17]

3) ***Broken by broken people:*** Hurting people hurt others. Wounded people pollute others. Psalm 55 records David's grief over a close friend's betrayal. Your heart may be broken not because of personal sin but the hurts afflicted on you by others. For example, your spouse's unfaithfulness can break and crush your heart.

If God will do a profound work in your heart and use you to touch others, you must be broken about your sinfulness or carnality and the deplorable state of your family, church, community, or nation.

What Type of Heart do you Have?

Human beings have different categories of hearts. As a believer who desires to progress spiritually with God, you must know your heart to collaborate with the Holy Spirit for your transformation. God does not impose change on us; He accompanies us through the change process we are determined to achieve.

1) *A hardened heart*: This unyielding heart adamantly rejects God's will. Your heart is hardened when you insist on going your way after God's will has been revealed to you. Pharaoh is a typically biblical figure with a hardened heart. Exodus tells us that six times he had a "Hardened heart." Exodus 7:13 says his "Heart grew hard" after he witnessed the deadly plagues. (Also see Jeremiah 5:23).

2) *A stony heart:* It is a dead heart that cannot know and do God's will. Some people are spiritually dead like a rock. They are not moved at all, no matter what God is saying and doing. Ezekiel tells us that God wants to remove our stony hearts (Ezekiel 11:19).

3) *A heart that is lifted:* This is a heart full of self-importance and self-sufficiency. In Deuteronomy 8:11-14, Moses warned the people of Israel about the dangers of becoming arrogant when they have been blessed materially. Nebuchadnezzar became arrogant after his extraordinary achievements. Daniel 5:20 says,
"But when his heart became arrogant and hardened with pride, he was deposed from his royal throne and stripped of his glory."
This type of proud heart always brings people disgrace and ruin.

4) *A perverse heart:* This heart is full of all forms of sexual immorality – adultery, fornication, homosexuality, etc. (Psalm 101:4; Proverbs 12:8).

5) *A wicked heart:* This heart causes others to suffer (Proverbs 26:23). It is prone to evil (Jeremiah 17:1).

6) ***A deceitful heart:*** This heart lies, dupes people, manipulates, pretends, and is unreliable (Jeremiah 17:19-20; Proverbs 17:20).

7) ***An unbelieving heart:*** This heart resists, argues, and corrupts the truth of God's Word (Hebrews 3:12). A Christian with such a heart despises wise and godly counsel; and gravitates away from believers who are committed to walking in God's ways.

8) ***A veiled heart:*** This heart is covered by spiritual darkness, orchestrated by Satan (2 Corinthians 3:3-4, 15). One with such a heart finds it difficult to understand God's Word. Some people who have spent decades in Church still reason like spiritual babes. Their hearts are dull in understanding (Matthew 13:15; 1 Corinthians 3:1-2).

Revival Begins With a Broken Heart

A broken heart is the first thing you need to be used by God. A broken heart is teachable, humble, sincere, soft, and easily penetrated by God's Word. Unfortunately, people consider anything broken as useless and good for the garbage can. Contrarily, in Scripture, God only uses broken individuals and things. For example, Jacob at Peniel (Genesis 32), Israel went through the wilderness, David was in the wilderness for twenty years before ascending the throne, John the Baptist remained in the wilderness for several years before his introduction as a national prophet to Israel (Luke 1:80), and Jesus Christ was broken on the cross to become the Savior of the world. Also, Gideon's 300 soldiers broke the pitchers for the release of God's power (Judges 7), Mary broke the alabaster box to release the perfume (John 12), and the bread of the Holy Communion must be broken to be useful (1 Corinthians 11:23-30).

God's people are ready for revival only when they are broken.

"The Lord is near to those who have a broken heart and saves such as have a contrite spirit" (Psalm 34:18).

Eugene Peterson interprets this verse in the Message as,

"If your heart is broken, you'll find God right there" (Psalm 34:18 MSG).

You are at the gate of revival when you become conscious of your spiritual bankruptcy and helplessness, and you begin to long for God's help and salvation from the depth of your heart.

The church urgently needs revival in this season. The Church has a lot of noise, but God's voice is rare. Christianity is gaining popularity but losing its glory. The quantity of prayer is rising, but the quality is dropping. People are more excited about praying for personal needs and comfort, not about God's will. We must realize that our greatest need is not physical but spiritual; that our most significant problem is not the devil but our deviation from God's path; that the greatest enemy of our destiny is our disobedience to God's will, not a certain agent of the devil; and that the tremendous breakthrough is not money, but discovering our purpose in Christ.

Until God's light shines on us and causes us to see that even though we are busy doing things for Him, He is not happy with our quality of life; that we preach to others what we do not practice; that our interest in ministry is not the souls of men but money and fame; that we worship Him with our lips, but our hearts are far from Him; and that He will punish our sins, we are doomed to perish in spiritual dryness. God can only pour water from high on the thirsty heart. O Lord, make us thirsty for you!

A Man With a Broken Heart

Several contemporaries of William Seymour, the man God used as a catalyst of the Azusa Street Revival, testified that he had a broken heart – a man fully surrendered to God. Frank Bartleman, his co-laborer and fellow leader at the Azusa Street Mission, described him by saying, "He was very plain, spiritual, and humble… Brother Seymour generally sat behind two empty shoe boxes, one on top of the other. He usually kept his head inside the top one during the meeting in prayer. There was no pride there."[18]

William H. Durham, a visiting pastor to Azusa Street, described Seymour, "He walks and talks with God. His power is in his weakness. He seems to maintain a helpless dependence on God and is as simple-hearted as a little child, and at the same time is so filled with God that you feel the love and power every time you get near him."[19]

How to Cultivate a Broken Heart

Jesus Christ's life portrays a classical model for cultivating a broken heart and a humble life. Anyone desiring to manifest God's glory must intentionally pursue Christ to become more like Him.

1. **Embrace the Cross:**

Brokenness is divinely achieved and not by human effort. You cannot break your heart to become who God wants you to be; you need His help. But note that I am not ignoring man's role in the process. In Proverbs 23:26, God says,

"My son, GIVE ME YOUR HEART, and let your eyes observe my ways."

This verse indicates we have a crucial role to play in the process of the transformation of our hearts. "GIVE" in the above verse means to "Release, submit, or surrender." God needs your full cooperation to change you. So instead of focusing on asking for material things from Him, open your heart and release your will to Him for purification and imparting spiritual virtues.

You should know that you quickly gain access to the things in God's hands when He has your heart. But if, on the contrary, you focus on the things in His hands and miss His heart, you will be struggling to get the physical stuff He supplies. I can freely release my bank code to my wife because of my heart connection with her. We don't release secrets and precious things to those whose hearts are not committed to us.

God's instrument for breaking the human heart is, Christ's cross. Jesus told His followers,

"If any of you wants to be my follower, YOU MUST GIVE UP YOUR OWN WAY, TAKE UP YOUR CROSS, AND FOLLOW ME" (Matthew 16:24).

Jesus' disciples understood this message clearly. They were used to seeing criminals on their way to be crucified, carrying their crosses, and going after the executioners. They understood that to take the cross and go after Jesus Christ meant death. They knew that becoming followers or disciples of Christ could cost their lives. It was clear to them that their call was about enjoying blessings and also suffering for the truth.

Embracing the cross is submitting to the law of death. There is no way the old can transit into the new without engaging the power of death. God multiplies everything in life through death.

This is what Jesus is dealing with in John 12:24.

> *"Unless a grain of wheat falls into the ground and dies, it remains alone; but if it dies, it produces much grain."*

There is no spiritual power without death, crown without the cross, or glory without Calvary. Jesus was not murdered or assassinated, so stop pitying Him. He voluntarily handed Himself to be crucified for our salvation. That is why He is our hero.

> *"Greater love has no one than this: to lay down one's life for one's friends" (John 15:13).*

So, to embrace the cross means to submit to God's will for your life, even if it demands suffering. The power of the cross is activated when you despise the easy path of the flesh and choose the difficult path of the Spirit to please God. For example, you decide to turn down a well-paid job because it compromises your biblical code of ethics and choose to suffer financial lack for a season to please Jesus Christ. You accept to lose a juicy job because you cannot sleep with a boss. You refuse an offer to marry a wealthy unbeliever and face rejection and insults from your family because you cannot compromise your faith. You miss an opportunity to make big cash because you deliberately decide not to lie or cheat. While the mockeries from family members and friends humiliate you in the eyes of people, Christ's cross, which you have embraced, is breaking and transforming your heart.

A crucified life says, "Whatever God has approved for me is excellent, no matter what people think." Jesus needs people with such a mentality to go to the mission fields to save souls. Sadly, most Christians want to serve God only where comfort is guaranteed. The believers who brought the Gospel to Africa had a sacrifice mentality. They were willing to perish preaching the Gospel. We must rededicate our lives, and please our Master Jesus Christ, at all costs.

2. Always Feel for Others:

Somebody said, "Compassion is a passion with a heart." If our passion for God is pure, compassion will flow from us toward the needy and vulnerable. It is unchristian to ignore the plight of the less privileged while enjoying spiritual blessings and affluence. If you truly have God's Spirit, your heart must be troubled whenever you go out. Moral decadence, social injustice, corruption, poverty, disease, and squalor continue. You can do one little thing to reduce someone's burden or misery.

Jesus demonstrated love through the compassion He manifested toward those in need. Unlike the Pharisees, who saw the people as a means of making a profit, Jesus gave His all to save and serve them.

> *"When he saw the crowds, he had compassion for them, because they were harassed and helpless, like sheep without a shepherd" (Matthew 9:36).*

Jesus accommodated the lepers, epileptic, lame, blind, insane, sinners, rich, poor, and all calibers of people who needed His help. He healed them, cast out devils from them, fed them, and taught them how to flourish in the Kingdom. Summarily, Jesus existed to bring positive changes to those hurting, oppressed, and needy around Him.

This is how God expects us to live wherever He has placed us. In Mathew 5:13-16, Jesus summarizes our purpose for existence:

> *"Let me tell you why you are here. YOU'RE HERE TO BE SALT-SEASONING that brings out the God-flavors of this earth... Here's another way to put it: YOU'RE HERE TO BE LIGHT, bringing out the God-colors in the world. God is not a secret to be kept. We're going public with this, as public as a city on a hill. If I make you light-bearers, you don't think I'm going to hide you under a bucket, do you? I'm putting you on a light stand. Now that I've put you there on a hilltop, on a light stand—shine! Keep open house; be generous with your lives. By opening up to others, you'll prompt people to open up with God, this generous Father in heaven" (MSG).*

Many Christians are looking for fancy prophecies about their destinies. Here is your prophecy! In the above text, Jesus clearly reveals why you exist. You are SALT and LIGHT! Your role is to find out how to live like salt and light in your workplace and community and begin to touch lives. This is the secret of unlocking the blessings God has promised for you. God prospers people who bless others.

Your heart will be broken and humbled when you continuously serve all those you meet because you understand that you are a product of God's grace. It is grace that brought you to where you are now. The treatment we receive from the public space these days is horrific. Most people driven by greed for money no longer value human beings; they only think about financial and material profit. Abuse has become very rampant. God expects believers, moved by the fear of God, to make a difference by serving people with compassion.

Several parents are agonizing because the children they invest a lot to raise have abandoned them. While on a trip abroad, I heard about a man who had helped over twenty people in that country, but none of his relatives was among them. What argument can you present before God that you have helped several others but not a single person from your family?

It is time to ask God to change our hearts and help us to feel for others, starting with our family members. As you go out daily, pray and ask God to empower you to treat others how you would like to be treated. Your heart will be broken.

3. Promptly Forgive others and Ask for Forgiveness:

The path of forgiveness plus reconciliation is the way to brokenness.

Your heart is broken whenever you are willing to forgive, let go, and engage in the process of restoring a shattered relationship. The heart is hardened when you reject the request for forgiveness from your offender. Some people say vehemently, "I cannot forgive you. Over my dead body." If you say so, then you will die with a sick heart. Others say they have forgiven their offender, but they raise several arguments about never communicating with them or giving them a second chance. Still, others will hardly say, "I am sorry." We call them Mr. Right or Madam Right.

Jesus Christ is our example. While agonizing on the cross, He forgave and prayed for His persecutors,

"Father, forgive them; for they do not know what they are doing" (Luke 23:34).

He didn't curse them, despite the excruciating pains they inflicted on Him. Jesus knew He existed for reconciliation, not condemnation. Before the cross, He had taught His disciples what to do with their persecutors in Matthew 5:43-44,

"You have heard that it was said, 'You shall love your neighbor and hate your enemy. But I say to you, Love your enemies and pray for those who persecute you."

Genuine Christianity emphasizes love, demonstrated through forgiveness and reconciliation. Unfortunately, forgiveness and reconciliation, which should be easy for God's children, are becoming very difficult. It is common to have a Christian boycott a reconciliatory meeting called by a pastor because they have vowed never to forgive the offender. Some people believe you can live like enemies here on Earth and become friends in Heaven. You will never meet in heaven if you cannot greet each other here.

These two verses shook my life as a young convert when I discovered them:

"For if you forgive others their trespasses, your heavenly Father will also forgive you, but if you do not forgive others their trespasses, neither will your Father forgive your trespasses" (Matthew 6:14-15).

"Follow peace with all men, and holiness, without which no man shall see the Lord" (Hebrews 12:14).

I learned two vital truths from these scriptures: (1) God will not forgive me if I refuse to forgive my offender. In other words, I become a noise maker before God when I close my heart against an offender. (2) I will not make heaven if I fail to reconcile with my offender. So, I must do everything possible to live peacefully with everybody.

Today, two believers live in the same house, pray individually, and attend the same church but do not greet themselves because of an offense. You find Christians who have relocated to other churches without resolving issues with their fellow believer. In several families, siblings are at war, quarreling over material things and ruining their souls with anger, curses, bitterness, hatred, and malice. We must bring our hearts back to the cross for God to plow them and make us into peacemakers. Jesus said,

"Blessed are the peacemakers: for they shall be called the children of God" (Matthew 5:9).

God's glory will explode in our families and churches when we are willing to pay any price to make peace with each other.

4. Cultivate Humility

Merriam's English Dictionary defines "Humility" as "The quality of having a modest or low view of one's importance." To become broken and useable in God's hands, you have to choose the way of humility. What is the way of humility? Philippians 2:5-11 brings out vital lessons on humility from Jesus' life.

> *"5 Let this mind be in you, which was also in Christ Jesus: 6 Who, being in the form of God, thought it not robbery to be equal with God: 7 But made himself of no reputation, and took upon him the form of a servant, and was made in the likeness of men: 8 And being found in fashion as a man, he humbled himself, and became obedient unto death, even the death of the cross. 9 Wherefore God also hath highly exalted him, and given him a name which is above every name: 10 That at the name of Jesus every knee should bow, of things in heaven, and things in earth, and things under the earth; 11 And that every tongue should confess that Jesus Christ is Lord, to the glory of God the Father."*

In this text, Paul emphasizes that a Christian should have the same mindset or attitude as Christ (vs. 5). In other words, the perspective about life should be like that of Christ. Jesus didn't cling to His deity but voluntarily accepted to take upon Himself humanity for our salvation. For God to become, man was an act of inexplicable humility. Not only did He accept the lower state of humanity, He became a servant and died as a criminal on the cross. This was humiliating. Jesus was driven by humility to do this.

God expects us to be driven by humility in how we relate to each other and do our work. He wants us to be willing to forget about our social status and come down to serve others. If Jesus Christ, the King of kings and Lord of lords, could humble himself and wash the feet of His followers, why should we feel too important to do menial jobs for Him?

The challenge the church is facing today is that many are trying to minister before God without the garment of humility. In Matthew 20:25, Jesus instructs us not to abuse authority like the worldly people. Instead, to serve in humility.

> *"You know that the rulers in this world lord it over their people, and officials flaunt their authority over those under them."*

He washed the Disciples' feet publicly and then said,

> *"If I then, your Lord and Teacher, have washed your feet, you also ought to wash one another's feet. For I have given you an example, that you also should do just as I have done to you" (John 13:14-15).*

Today, some people are trying to borrow worldly methods to do God's work. We are not worldly celebrities; we are Kingdom servants. Let us carry and dispense the treasures of grace deposited in us by God in all humility. Never forget that God rejects the proud but gives abundant grace to the humble (James 4:6).

Deliberately choose the path of humility. Accept to do ministry without pay, expecting your reward from God. Accept low places presented to you with joy. Be quick to serve, not demanding others to serve you. Should titles and human praise blow your head? Refuse to be venerated by people because of your success. Always return all the glory to Jesus Christ, your Master.

In Search for Broken Vessels

Brokenness is an indispensable quality God needs in you to use you as an agent of revival and restoration. Brokenness is a divine work requiring your consecration and dedication to God. This message is therefore, a call for you to submit to the Holy Spirit for a profound work of transformation in your life. Let every challenge you are facing become a school for your spiritual formation. Let every satanic attack against you become a training ground for spiritual empowerment.

God is also calling you to intentionally focus on following Jesus Christ in His steps. This is a sure strategy to learn how to live a humble and simple life. Jesus Christ is our model and mentor. Grace to live for God flows as you gaze at Him continuously. Answer the call today; God will handle the rest! He is our model and mentor.

PRAYER POINTS
1. *Father, thank You for the revival You are activating in our midst in this season.*
2. *Father, thank You for the transformation taking place in my life, in Jesus' name.*

3. Father, thank You for the work of renewal and restoration taking place in my life, in Jesus' name.
4. Father, thank You for the incubation of the Holy Spirit in my family and the Church this season, in Jesus' name.
5. Father, thank You for revealing deep things to me on this mountain, in Jesus' name.
6. Father, thank You for the ministry of angels in my life and family this season, in Jesus' name.
7. Father, thank You because You are close to the broken-hearted; You will do more extraordinary things in my life, in Jesus' name.
8. Holy Spirit, take over my heart and change it the way You want, in Jesus' name.
9. Father, release Your fire in my heart and dismantle every evil rule of anger, jealousy, envy, lust, covetousness, hate, pride, etc., in Jesus' name.
10. Father, You know the things You don't like in my life; reveal them to me and help me to deal with them, in Jesus' name.
11. Father, pour out Your Spirit and convict us of sin, in Jesus' name.
12. Father, arise and rebuke the Church of wickedness and compromise, in Jesus' name.
13. Father, arise and expose wickedness in the Church, in Jesus' name.
14. Father, reveal to us once more what the Church is supposed to look like, in Jesus' name.
15. Father, pour out Your Spirit on us and give us the grace to repent of evil, in Jesus' name.
16. Father, break my heart, mold it, and make it pure for Your glory, in Jesus' name.
17. Go to the section on the different types of hearts and pray against an evil heart.
18. Father, give me a willing and obedient heart, in Jesus' name.
19. Father, fill my heart with Your Spirit and cause me to think like Christ, in Jesus' name.
20. Father, deliver me from self-centeredness and greed and help me to see the needs of others, in Jesus' name.
21. O Lord Jesus Christ, increase in me as I decrease, in Jesus' name.
22. Father, deliver me of every poison of pride and arrogance in Jesus' name.
23. Father, teach me the way of brokenness and humility, in Jesus' name.
24. Fire of God, fall in our Church; expose and destroy the works of witchcraft and occultism, in Jesus' name.
25. Father, arise and break the powers of principalities and powers manipulating the Church in this nation, in Jesus' name.

26. Father, arise, expose, and deliver Your children from the networks of false prophets, in Jesus' name.
27. Father, I embrace the cross and submit to Your will for my life, in Jesus' name.
28. Father, give me a heart that forgives continuously.
29. Father, teach me the way of humility, in Jesus' name.
30. Are there some people you must forgive or reconcile with? Decide on what to do and do it now.
31. Father, arise today for the reconciliation of broken marriages and families, in Jesus' name.
32. Father, touch the hearts of believers to be moved by what is going wrong in the churches and the society.
33. Father, arise and restore salt and light in the Church, in Jesus' name.
34. Father, deliver me from every trace of pride and arrogance that leads to destruction, in Jesus' name.
35. Father, teach me how to hide and flourish, in Jesus' name.
36. Arise, O Lord, and cut off every power of Herod released from hell against my life, in Jesus' name.
37. Father, arise and rescue my children from every power of Herod released from hell against their destinies, in Jesus' name.
38. Father, frustrate the plans of agents of darkness assigned by hell to destroy God's servants in this nation, in Jesus' name.
39. Fire of God, fall now and stir intercessors to pray for this nation.
40. O Lord, baptize me with a burden to labor for the salvation of my family, in Jesus' name.
41. Father, release Your fire on the Church and release mighty apostles, prophets, evangelists, pastors, and teachers to restore your glory in the Church.
42. Father, arise and cut off every hand fighting revival in this nation.
43. Father, deliver Your servants from distraction and confusion, in Jesus' name.
44. Father, pour out Your Spirit and raise agents of reconciliation in every family, Church, and nation, in Jesus' name.
45. Father, humble world leaders who are boasting against You and cause multitudes to discover the power of the living God, in Jesus' name.
46. Father, arise in my life and break the powers that want to keep me on the ground, in Jesus' name.
47. Father, arise and destroy the powers standing against the emergence of the righteous in this nation, in Jesus' name.

48. *Father, arise and destroy satanic bondages hindering our nation's spiritual and economic progress, in Jesus' name.*
49. *Father, fill the hearts of Your children in the positions of power to become agents of transformation, in Jesus' name.*
50. *Present Your needs to the Lord and conclude with thanksgiving.*

Chapter 4
Days 10-12

A Thankful Heart

"In everything give thanks; for this is the will of God in Christ Jesus for you" (1 Thessalonians 5:18).

Thankfulness is a key that gives us access to God's power and men's hearts. Ingratitude and ungratefulness shut the heavens and scare people away from us. Incessantly, barriers break, mountains crumble, and problems melt before thanksgivers because they never lack God's anointing. One who is full of gratitude is never embarrassed because they constantly attract destiny helpers. The Spirit of thanksgiving is an indispensable requirement in the life of an agent of revival.

How I Discovered the Power in the Blood of Jesus

Before I became a disciple of Jesus Christ in November 1993, I had messed up my mind with pornographic materials. This made my early days in the faith challenging because the devil kept harassing my mind with unclean thoughts and images. One day the Holy Spirit taught me a vital lesson. He inspired me to use the blood of Jesus as a weapon against evil thoughts and demonic harassment. Consequently, whenever the devil shot a strange thought into my mind like an arrow, I quickly declared, "The blood of Jesus." I realized that whenever I pleaded for the blood of Jesus, the negative thought vanished like a bubble in the air. Hallelujah! What a discovery!

So, every day, I pleaded for the blood of Jesus several times. There were moments I did it quietly in my mind, and it still worked. I began applying it to strange dreams too. Sometimes during my sleep, I was attacked by evil forces, pressing me down; as soon as I woke up, I would start pleading for the blood of Jesus. God's peace flooded my heart all the times I did that. I have not stopped using this weapon till today. The good news is that it is always available for you too.

How I Discovered the Power of Thankfulness

As time passed, the Holy Spirit revealed another weapon to me – "Thank you, Jesus!" I found in the Bible 1 Thessalonians 5:18, which says, *"In everything give thanks to God..."* I understood it to mean that I have to thank Jesus for everything that happens to me. So, I began to apply it, and it worked wonderfully for me, and it is still working now. For example, when walking and hitting my foot against an object, I first say, "Thank you, Jesus!" When an insect flies into my eye, I say, "Thank you, Jesus!" Whatever happens, I say, "Thank you, Jesus," before thinking about what to do. "Thank you, Jesus," ultimately became a reflex in me. I would say it before trying to comprehend what had happened.

I came to believe, and I teach that if the devil enters my house physically, I would first say, "Thank you, Jesus," before I deal with him. I believe whatever he meant evil for me will work for my good. Also, God would have kept him away from my house if I couldn't deal with him.

What I have been experiencing through thanking Jesus in unpleasant circumstances is peace, self-control, and wisdom to respond to challenging situations. Often, when the devil launches an attack against us, his primary goal is to destabilize and cause us to doubt God or become bitter against Him. He wants to activate bitterness and discouragement in your spirit to gain access to your life. But if your first reaction to pain and adversity is thanksgiving to God, you give the devil a technical knockout. "Thank you, Jesus!"

Why Being Thankful is Imperative

Thankfulness is a key that gives you access to God's presence and power. Thanksgivers always have the anointing. Gratitude is a key to people's hearts. A grateful person never lacks destiny helpers.

1. A Thankful Heart is Key to Divine Presence:

A thankful heart is full of divine presence and power. To be full of thanks is to be full of God. David speaks about this from experience.

> *"But You are holy, Enthroned in the praises of Israel" (Psalm 22:3).*

God establishes His throne/headquarters where He is praised. Only a thankful heart can give God meaningful praise. Friend, you can establish God's headquarter in your life and home through your praises.

> *"Enter into His gates with thanksgiving, And into His courts with praise. Be thankful to Him, and bless His name" (Psalm 100:4).*

The Message simplifies it.

> *"Enter with the password: "Thank you!" Make yourselves at home, talking praise. Thank him. Worship him" (Psalm 100:4).*

I exclaimed, "Woah!" when I first read this. I said to myself, "So Thanksgiving is a password?" I will constantly use it. Friend, thanksgiving is a secret code God has given us to access His presence.

Those who will flow with the Spirit of revival know how to activate God's power through thanksgiving.

2. Thanksgiving is a Weapon of Warfare:

Thanksgiving, celebration, and prophetic worship are weapons of spiritual warfare. Joshua and Israel conquered Jericho with shouts of praise (Joshua 6). God revealed the same strategy to King Jehoshaphat, who was confronted by three foreign armies. The Israelites praised God, and their enemies went into a rampage and began slaughtering themselves (2 Chronicles 20). Years later, Paul and Silas unconsciously detonated the weapon of praise and thanksgiving in a Prison in Philippi, and chains were broken to pieces (Acts 16). The power released by their praise caused an earthquake. Can you imagine that?

We must understand how to deploy the weapons of thanksgiving, praise, and prophetic worship as we engage the forces of darkness in warfare for deliverance, revival, and restoration in our families, communities, and nations. A praise giver cannot be pressed down.

3. A Thankful Heart is a Medicine:

You absolutely need thankfulness in difficult times as medicine for your preservation and restoration. The Bible says so in Proverbs 17:22:

"A cheerful heart is good medicine. But a broken spirit dries the bones."

The Good News says,

"Being cheerful keeps you healthy. It is slow death to be gloomy all the time."

While gratitude heals and restores us, sorrow dries the bones. Ingratitude is a slow death. In the above verse, the Bible connects bone diseases to sorrow. Health experts say osteoporosis (Bone disease) is a major public health threat. Multiple studies have reported a connection between depression and low bone density. Depression induces bone loss and osteoporotic fractures.[20] According to experts, other health problems caused by prolonged anger, bitterness, and ingratitude are headache, digestion problems, abdominal pain, insomnia, increased anxiety, depression, high blood pressure, skin problems (Such as eczema.), heart attack, etc. This is why you must declare war against depression and a moody lifestyle. The most effective weapon to use is "Thanksgiving and worship." Keep saying, "Thank you, Jesus!"

Remember Rick Warren's counsel, "Happy moments, PRAISE GOD. Difficult moments, SEEK GOD. Quiet moments, WORSHIP GOD. Painful moments, TRUST GOD. Every moment, THANK GOD."

4. Thankfulness Draws People to Christ:

Around us, people are sinking daily into sorrow, depression, and gloominess. Today, as you go out there, take time and observe the faces of those you meet. You will see a cloud of despair hanging over some people's faces, confusion on others, and a dark veil of bitterness on some few. You may be shocked to find only a few happy and enthusiastic people.

As God's children, we are called to inspire hope everywhere we go, through the perfume of the joy of the Holy Ghost, flowing from us.

"He uses us to spread the knowledge of Christ everywhere, like a sweet perfume" (2 Corinthians 2:14).

I read this story somewhere. A lady was crossing a certain London station when an old man stopped her and said, "Excuse me, ma'am, I want to thank you for something." "Thank me?" exclaimed the lady. "Yes. I used to be a ticket collector, and whenever you went by, you always gave me a cheerful smile and a good morning, and you don't know the difference it made to me. Wet or fine, it was always the same, and I think to myself, 'I Wonder where she gets her smile from. One cannot always be happy, yet she seems to be, and I knew that the smile must come from inside somehow. Then one morning, you came by with a little Bible in your hand, and I said to myself, perhaps that is where she got her smile from. So, I went home that night and bought a Bible, and I've been reading it, and I have found Christ, and now I can smile too, and I want to thank you."

Like the woman in this story, we are responsible for spreading the joy we have received. And the most excellent way to spread our joy is to lead emotionally battered people to our source, Jesus Christ.

Thanking God is a key to releasing His power into our lives. Whenever you turn on the praise button, the door of the supernatural opens in your life. I agree with Rick Warren, who says, "Every moment, thank God!"

Many Christians have not yet discovered the divine power released when we thank God in all circumstances. The Holy Spirit taught me this secret when I was a few months old in the faith, as I mentioned earlier. I keep thanking God for such a glorious revelation that has continuously helped me enjoy His power all these years.

5. **Thankfulness Leads to Generosity:**

A thankful heart is generous – passionate about sharing. Ungrateful people are greedy and stingy because everything looks small in their eyes. If our hearts are full of gratitude for God's abundant love and mercies, we will always be willing to share whatever good thing we have with others.

Generosity is not about how much we have in our hands but how much love our heart has. Some say, "I will be generous when I become very wealthy." No! You will be generous when your heart is full of love. If your heart has love, you will add value to people's lives with the little you have. If you cannot bless people with the little you have now, you may not do so when you have abundance.

Research from the Institute of Social Change showed that in the United Kingdom, a few years ago, the poorest 20% gave 3.2% of their income to charity. In comparison, the wealthiest 20% gave 0.9%. Financial expert Daniel Levin says, "Prosperity isn't in what you've attained, but rather in what you give away." Having much does not guarantee generosity. It is abundant gratitude in our hearts that does.

One day, a lady in our church I knew to have an ungrateful attitude visited us and met me, parceling some books I had brought from the printing press. She asked me for a free copy. Before I could react, my brother, who had come in from the U.S.A., pulled out some money from his pocket and gave her to buy a copy of my new book for herself. Surprisingly, this lady slotted the money into her purse and insisted I give her the book for free.

Ungratefulness is a breeding ground for greed and stinginess. It will rub you of opportunities to be blessed and become a blessing to others. Shun it!

How to Cultivate a Thankful Heart

Your heart is a vessel. Whatever you allow to pour into it will contaminate your life. Whatever you permit to dwell in, it will build or break you. So, fill your heart with the following to be thankful all the time:

1. Remember Where God Has Picked You:

You will not be ungrateful and disenchanted if you remember where God's mercy and grace picked you. Ungrateful people often forget how far God has brought them. In Deuteronomy 6:12, Moses warned the children of Israel against the danger of forgetting where God brought them.

> *"Take care lest you forget the LORD, who brought you out of the land of Egypt, out of the house of slavery."*

Were you poor before, and today you are very wealthy? Always remember how God's grace has lifted you, and be thankful. Never allow success to fill your head and make you pompous. Bragging will bring you down. Stay simple, humble, and thankful to God.

2. Count Your Blessings:

You will be grateful if you fix your eyes on the good things God has done. Focusing on the negative side of life will sap you of your spiritual energy and leave you bitter and depressed. David was a man who constantly faced multi-faceted attacks. His life was a mixture of sweet and bitter days. In Psalm 103:2, he teaches us a vital lesson on self-motivation and thankfulness.

"Bless the LORD, O my soul, and forget not all his benefits." Each time you forget God's benefits, you are buried in sorrow. Hence, start counting your blessings every day you wake up. Make up your mind to focus on what is good, godly, and excellent.

Reject the "I am cursed mentality." If you are born again, then Christ has redeemed you from every curse (Galatians 3:13). If you are living in Christ, then you have been blessed with all spiritual blessings in heavenly places (Ephesians 1:3). While you are working toward improving on your physical condition, keep reminding yourself that you are blessed. Unfortunately, most Christians believe they are cursed. Listen to what God has said and not what Satan is saying. In Christ, you are blessed! Be thankful!

3. Focus on God's Promises:

A believer whose mind is focused on God's glorious promises is always thankful. How can you be sure of your future and be frustrated simultaneously? On the contrary, those whose minds are not saturated with God's promises are confused, fearful, and constantly anxious.

There are thousands of promises in the Bible telling us what God will do for those who love Him. In 1 Corinthians 2:9, Paul writes that human imagination cannot figure out the glorious things God has prepared for those who love him. God's promises guarantee the great future God has designed for you.

In consonant with this, we see how Jesus constantly tapped into the riches of heaven by using the key of thanksgiving as He focused on His Father's promises. In Matthew 15:36, all He did to multiply the bread and fish with which he fed five thousand men was "Thank you, Father…" At Lazarus' tomb, He thanked His Father, then called forth the dead man to life.

"Father, I thank you that you have heard me. I knew that you always hear me…" (John 11:41-42).
Jesus is thankful because He trusts in the faithfulness of His Father.

God has promised us a revival in this season. Let us focus on the promise as we defy the odds in prayer, fasting, soul-winning, discipleship, church planting, and missions. Fill your heart with God's promises so that you can always see the possibility in adversity. Meditate on God's promises, and your heart will continuously appreciate His goodness.

4. Decide to be Positive:

Being grateful or ungrateful is a choice. Paul wants us to choose to be thankful no matter the circumstance when he says,

"Do not be anxious about anything, but in everything by prayer and supplication with thanksgiving let your requests be made known to God" (Philippians 4:6).

The first thing to do to live a thankful life is, to be positive. Tell yourself, "I will not accommodate toxic emotions like hatred, unforgiveness, envy, jealousy, etc." Second, decide to appreciate little things. Don't wait for big things to happen for you to be excited. Live like cats who get excited with the last thing you give them. Tell yourself, "I will not be ungrateful. I will always appreciate people. I will thank God for the little I have while waiting for bigger things." Third, perform random acts of kindness. You become more thankful when you serve others. So, intentionally show kindness to people. Give tips to those who serve you. God went the extra mile to serve and make somebody happy. Your joy will multiply.

You will undoubtedly face challenges as you accomplish God's assignment for your life. You will be unstoppable if, like Apostle Paul, you choose to be positive even in chains (Acts 16:25-31).

5. Surround Yourself With Grateful People:

Negative people in your life drain you, the wrong people derail you, while bitter people break you. You must constantly identify such people and weed them from your life. While writing this chapter, I got a call from an unknown man requesting prayer for his wife, who had deserted her home. When I asked him why his wife left him, he told me frankly that it was the influence of bad friends. Sadly, some adults do not know how to discern and discard negative people from their lives.

The Bible is clear,

"Don't be fooled: "Bad friends will ruin good habits" (1 Corinthians 15:33 ERV).

Negative people cannot motivate you to be grateful to God. They corrupt your soul through gossip, complaining, murmuring, hate, criticism, and cursing. Root them out of your life. On the contrary, you overflow with joy and gratitude when surrounded by people who make you happy, remind you of God's goodness, appreciate you, and pray with you. Connect to such people.

The days are evil. You don't have time to waste around people not going anywhere. Folks who are ignorant that to follow and please Jesus Christ, is a race we must win and a battle we must conquer. Team up with believers bent on making heaven and creating an impact while they exist here on earth. They will help you live a fulfilled and thankful life.

Begin to Use the Weapon of Thanksgiving

Thanksgiving is a lethal weapon against the forces of darkness because it brings God's presence and power into every battle you face. Thanksgiving is also a key that opens mysterious doors. A pastor who died and was later resuscitated explained how he saw angels open doors through Thanksgiving without touching them when he got to heaven.

Decide to become a thanks-giver through prayer, praise, and releasing your precious gifts to God. Also, constantly appreciate those who show you kindness. Always ask God to fill your mouth with a new song to praise Him.

Praise-givers and worshipers are carriers of God's glory. If you use Thanksgiving effectively, you will become a catalyst of revival everywhere you go. Praise the Lord!

PRAYER POINTS

1. *Give thanks to God today for the glorious experiences you have been having since you started praying with this book.*
2. *Father, thank You because my life will never remain the same.*
3. *Thank God for every challenge you are going through; it is not your destination.*
4. *Thank God for every member of your family and all He has been doing in their lives.*
5. *Count your blessings, name them one by one, and praise God.*
6. *Ask God for an anointing of praise and thanksgiving in your life.*
7. *Father, thank You for the gift of the blood of Jesus.*
8. *Father, thank You for the wonder-working power in the blood of Jesus Christ.*
9. *Father, thank You for the gift of Your Word and its wonders in my life.*

10. Father, thank You for the power in the name of Jesus in my life.
11. Father, thank You for the power of Your grace that has saved me and made me who I am.
12. Father, thank You for not allowing my enemies to destroy me.
13. Father, thank You for giving me victory in trials and temptations.
14. Father, thank You for healing me of deadly diseases.
15. Father, thank You for making me a member of Your family in Christ.
16. Father, thank You for Your grace that has canceled disgrace in my life.
17. Father, thank You for giving me favor with friends and strangers.
18. Father, thank You for the glorious destiny I have in Christ.
19. Father, thank You because every good work You have started in my life will be perfected.
20. Father, thank You because You will turn my darkness to light, fill my emptiness, and restore order in my life.
21. Father, thank You because I will fulfill my days and not perish with the wicked.
22. Father, thank You because every hidden talent in me will manifest in Jesus' name.
23. Father, thank You for restoring the things Satan has stolen from my life.
24. Father, thank You because I have conquered the serpent in Christ, and I am unbeatable, in Jesus' name.
25. Father, thank You because the voice of the blood of Jesus Christ in my life is more potent than every evil force speaking against me.
26. Father, thank You because I am safe under the blood of Jesus Christ.
27. Father, thank You because my ministry will increase from glory to glory by the power of the Holy Spirit, in Jesus' name.
28. Father, thank You because I am not alone; You will see me through every trial, in Jesus' name.
29. Father, thank You because I will not sing the song of defeat in Your house.
30. Father, thank You because Your angel of security will never leave me, in Jesus' name.
31. Father, thank You because my health and prosperity give You pleasure.
32. Father, thank You because Your anointing will restore perfect unity in my family, in Jesus' name.
33. Father, thank You because even though my beginning is small, my end will be great, in Jesus' name.
34. Father, thank You because whatever my enemies have prepared against me will work for me, in Jesus' name.

35. *Father, thank You because I am coming out of every prison or limitation stronger, in Jesu's name.*
36. *Father, thank You because what did not stop Jesus Christ cannot stop me, in Jesus' name.*
37. *Father, thank You because, from today, I am stepping into my new level, in Jesus' name.*
38. *Father, thank You because my enemies will honor me, in Jesus' name.*
39. *Father, thank You because no one will take my place, in Jesus' name.*
40. *Father, thank You because I am part of the great work You are doing in the end time Church, in Jesus' name.*
41. *Father, thank You because Your counsel will abide on my house and illuminate my family for great things, in Jesus' name.*
42. *Father, thank You because I am not leaving this mountain empty-handed.*
43. *Father, thank You because I will be hidden in the rock in the day of disaster, in Jesus' name.*
44. *Father, thank You because rivers of living water flow out of my belly.*
45. *Father, thank You because You will give me the territories of my enemies for Your glory.*
46. *Father, thank You for choosing me as a platform to reveal Your power to the world.*
47. *Father, thank You because my head will never lack Your oil.*
48. *Father, thank You because small things will increase in my hands, and dead things will live, in Jesus' name.*
49. *Father, thank You because we will see Your glory abundantly in this nation.*
50. *Father, thank You for the wind of revival blowing in this land.*
51. *Spend time today praising and worshipping God for Who He is and what He has done.*

Chapter 5
Days 13-15

A Heart Full of Love

"Do everything in love" (1 Corinthians 16:14).

An atmosphere of love is where God's power operates fully. Thus, to walk in love is to work with God. Working in division, competition, envy, and jealousy is working without God. Therefore, it is incumbent on us to make an unrelated effort to cultivate a climate of love around each of our families, communities, churches, and nations through which God's power can operate mighty works among us. As long as we continue to tolerate unforgiveness, tribalism, hatred, injustice, partiality, and abuse in our midst, we are not ready for revival and restoration. God wants to pour His Spirit of love into hearts for a mighty work.

How God Taught me to Preserve an Atmosphere of Love in my Home

I woke up at 3am quaking with fear, and the Holy Spirit's voice spoke crystal clear, "Never sleep with bitterness in your heart if you want your marriage and ministry to survive in this place." This was barely two days after we had arrived at our new pastoral station in Foumbot, West Region – Cameroon. That night, I had gone to bed very bitter and demoralized because of my misunderstanding with my wife and the baptism of fire I was experiencing in the new station.

My small family of four – my wife and I, our first son Praise, and Margret, my wife's kid sister, arrived in Foumbot in April 2001 to serve a church that had not been prepared to receive the new pastor. Consequently, no church member came to welcome us. Unfortunately, all we had as funds for food and basic needs was less than five thousand francs ($8). We ran out of food and essential family needs within a few days. I recall how our young son, Praise, cried for a long time because he was hungry, but we had no money to buy biscuits for him. My wife, pregnant with our second daughter Phoebe was also starving.

The atmosphere in the house was volatile for squabbles. Hunger and the feelings of rejection had dried up love from my heart. I eventually had a misunderstanding with my wife, which caused me to go to bed bitter. I didn't care to empty my heart and pray with my family that evening. In fact, I ignored her and went to bed.

At around 3am that night, I had a horrific dream that shook me. A strange, dreadful serpent violently attacked me. I began to struggle to kill it but realized that I could not because I did not have a weapon nor the strength to withstand it. When things were going out of hand, my younger brother James Tangumonkem unexpectedly came to the scene with a sword and struck the serpent to death. Instantly, I woke up from sleep, frightened. I began to pray immediately and asked God what was going on. He told me bitterness in my heart, and discouragement had opened the door to the spirits of the land to attack us. He warned me that if I did not root them out, my ministry in Foumbot would fail woefully.

Attacked by the Spirits of the Land

I had visited Foumbot town earlier to survey and spiritually map the land. Amazingly, I found out that the symbol of the Bamoun tribe was a double-head serpent. I understood that a serpentine spirit influenced the territory. That night, the Holy Spirit helped me to realize that the spirits of the land were confronting me.

Because of the state of my heart, I found myself spiritually unfit to strike the evil forces of the land. Confronted with this truth, I repented before the Lord that night and asked my wife to forgive me. We reconciled, and I resolved that night never to go to sleep with bitterness in my heart again. By God's grace, I have done my best to live by that decision to date.

I remember an incident of disagreement in our next station, Bamenda, in 2003. That night, I reminded my wife that we couldn't sleep until we resolved the issue. From 9pm that evening till 3am, we sat on our bed in the room, dosing and talking until we arrived at a peaceful conclusion before going to sleep. Praise God!

Phyllis Diller, a renowned American comedian, in her book *"House Keeping Hints,"* said, "Never go to bed mad; stay up and fight." Well, that's a comedian's counsel. Instead, you should follow our example; stay up and dialogue!

By God's grace, resolving our differences before we sleep has become a golden rule for our marriage; we don't sleep with any unsettled issues. Don't carry anger to sleep!

Don't give Satan a chance

Any time you consciously or unconsciously open the door to Satan, you will suffer the painful consequences. For this reason, the Bible warns us in Ephesians 4:26-27 not to give the devil a foothold in our lives.

"In your anger, do not sin. Do not let the sun go down while you are still angry, and do not give the devil a foothold" (NIV).

In this verse, we can identify three sins that give the devil free access to your life and home: anger, bitterness, and unforgiveness. (1) Anger is your reaction to maltreatment or hurt. (2) Bitterness is the feelings you generate when you fail to deal with your hurt. (3) Unforgiveness is the refusal to let go of the hurt when you have the opportunity to do so. Paul warns us that these toxic emotions can give Satan access to our lives.

The word translated in the above verse as "Foothold" comes from the Greek word, *'Topos.'* It is the root word for topography, meaning "Home, opportunity, or license." This implies the devil takes control of someone because he has been given a license, opportunity, or space to do so. Take this counsel from Joyce Meyer seriously. "Never go to bed angry. I don't know about you, but I'm glad this verse is in the Bible."

Generally, couples treat offenses in their marriages differently: (1) They try to ignore the problem and die in silence. (2) They engage in dialogue to resolve it. (3) They decide to separate homes or divorce. Let me underline that every marital problem can be resolved if the parties are willing. I have witnessed reconciliation between couples facing various marital crises like adultery, incest, abandonment, violence, etc. I have seen a husband forgive and welcome back home his wife who had committed adultery with his best friend.

One day a man brought his two daughters to my office in Bamenda from Mamfe for deliverance prayer. While I began praying for them, the Holy Spirit told me that the demonic attack in their lives was the problem the man had had with his wife. When I asked him to see his wife, he told me she had left the marriage more than thirteen years before and was based in Kumba. By this time, she had given birth to a child out of wedlock. God worked out a miraculous reconciliation between the two of them. The man's family was excited and sent a delegation to go to Kumba and bring back his wife home. The day she returned, the husband called me on the phone, and I could hear great jubilation in the background.

"Never go to bed angry. Now I don't know about you, but I'm glad this verse is in the Bible."

Revival is the Restoration of God's Love

Revival happens when God's people begin to love Him passionately and fellow man compassionately. The outpour of the Holy Spirit in hearts produces this experience. In Mark 12:30-31, Jesus summarizes how God expects us to love.

> *"And you shall love the Lord your God with all your heart and with all your soul and with all your mind and with all your strength.' The second is this: 'You shall love your neighbor as yourself.' There is no other commandment greater than these."*

In John 13:34, Jesus emphasizes a new commandment we must live by as Christians.

> *"A new commandment I give to you, that you love one another; as I have loved you, that you also love one another" (John 13:34).*

The Holy Spirit is at work to see God's purpose, which is love, unity, and peace prevail among His people. Christianity without love is like a painted fire that cannot burn – it doesn't impact the world. Christ's church becomes a laughing stock when His children cannot manifest His love to one another and the non-believers.

Loving God

We must restore God's love in our hearts to become agents of positive societal impact. Christianity without sincere and sacrificial love for Jesus Christ is noisy and powerless. Several portions of Scripture confirm that a Christian can be religious but not spiritual. This means you can be a good preacher but a bad practitioner.

The story of the Church in Ephesus, recorded in Revelation 2:1-7, reveals that the first thing Jesus Christ expects from us is sincere LOVE for Him, not our religious activities. That is why He sharply rebuked the hyperactive Christians in Ephesus.

> *"Nevertheless, I have this against you, THAT YOU HAVE LEFT YOUR FIRST LOVE" (Revelation 2: 4).*

Scrutinizing Revelation 2:1-3 reveals eight signs indicating that the Ephesians were busy with church activities. But one thing was lacking: they had lost their first love and dedication to Jesus Christ. We find this same situation in the Church today. There is zeal for realizing big projects for the Kingdom, but what the Lord Jesus Christ values most is missing: the tender and fervent love for HIM. You may ask, "Is it possible to serve God without loving him?" The answer is YES! Revelation 2:4 in the New Living Translation brings light to this:

> *"But I have this complaint against you. You DON'T LOVE ME OR EACH OTHER AS YOU DID AT FIRST!"*

It is possible to serve in Church while living in open or secret sin. You can sing well in the choir while you don't greet your fellow choir member because of an unresolved offense. You can gradually backslide into lies-telling, manipulation, pride, nepotism, immorality, division, etc., but continue serving zealously. Some Christians are committed to doing things in Church but do not spend quality time to fellowship with Jesus Christ and find out His perfect will for their lives. Why all this busyness with religious activities without a profound love for Jesus Christ? Serving in the Church may have some economic returns. Financial and material benefits may become your motivation for service. This can become a trap for your soul. Ask yourself, "Why am I serving God?" Is it to please Him or for the benefit?

Ministry in the church could become a stage performance in which you sing, preach, and teach to people without genuine love for God or the people. As a professional, you don't need a heart full of love to perform. You can do it well in the flesh without the anointing because you have sharpened your skills. I read about a Psychiatric doctor who used to refer patients to a comedian to make them laugh and relieve their emotional problems. One day the comedian went to consult the doctor. "I will send you to the best comedian in town, and your problem will be solved through laughter." Surprisingly, the patient said, "I am the comedian." Have you become a professional entertainer in God's house, ministering without life? Don't be deceived by your sweet voice. What transforms people is the quality of life you transmit during your ministration, not the sweet melody that moves them emotionally. Sadly, some people minister for entertainment, not transformation. God has not called us to be entertainers. We are ministers of life. The Holy Spirit wants to rekindle the fire of Christ's love in our hearts. Catch that fire now in Jesus' name.

Beloved in the Lord, Jesus Christ came from heaven to love us with the same love with which the Father loved Him (John 17:26). He suffered and died for us to draw our hearts unto Himself for the experience of this dimension of love. His heart can be satisfied with nothing less than a deep and personal love for Him flowing from our hearts. As you desire a deep and fresh passion for Jesus, I pray that the Holy Spirit will fill your heart and draw you closer to Him more and more.

Loving Fellow-man

LOVE is the true mark of genuine Christianity. Loving God always results in loving fellow man. The inability to express love to others as Christians discredits our faith. Have you ever witnessed a Christian manifest callousness and wickedness towards a fellow believer or a non-believer? It is disheartening. Even non-believers judge it abnormal. I have sat for several hours trying to reconcile Christian couples to no avail, and the question I often ask is, "Where is God's love in their hearts?" I have experienced that it is very easy to reconcile people whose hearts are ruled by God's love. It is like trying to pour sand into a bottle. On the contrary, it is an extremely tough assignment to reconcile carnal or unrepentant people whose hearts lack God's love. It is like trying to force gravel into a bottle.

The standard for our love for others is the love Jesus has demonstrated toward us. He says,

> *"A new commandment I give to you, that you LOVE ONE ANOTHER; AS I HAVE LOVED YOU, that you also love one another" (John 13:34).*

If you understand this verse, you will realize that loving others as Jesus Christ wants goes beyond what society has taught us. The love He is talking about is divinely empowered love, the God-kind of love – *Agape love* (sacrificial love). Most people love others when they have a good reason to do so. You would agree that loving those who have manifested kindness to you is easy. You don't have to pray and fast to love someone who gives you money monthly or speaks well about you to everybody. We readily give to and associate with those who give us things.

Now, loving those who are not kind to us like Jesus Christ wants is challenging. Our flesh hates it. Do you easily give to those who cannot pay you back? How do you treat those who hate, criticize, castigate, and lie against you? Human nature would say, "Pay them back in their coins." Even though it is not easy, Jesus wants us to love them because God loves and wants to save them.

Here is the secret: loving others is easy when you sincerely love and imitate Jesus Christ in all you do. He told His disciples that He loved them as the Father had loved Him. If you refuse to fully surrender to Jesus Christ's will as the King of your life, you cannot trample on your ego and love your enemies (Matthew 5:44; 1 Corinthians 13:1-8; Luke 23:34). There are dimensions of blessings we will not experience as individuals, families, communities, and nation until we engage love at this level of pardoning our enemies and giving them a second chance. We are saved today because Jesus decided to love us, His enemies, and come down to save us.

We urgently need the restoration of divine love in our hearts. Many hearts are dry spiritually due to offenses, the pressures of life, and demonic attacks. The result is the proliferation of conflicts in homes, churches, communities, and nations. The cure to all conflicts is, God's love. Peace will prosper and multiply in our midst as God's love prevails in our hearts. O Lord, baptize us today with your kind of love!

How to Cultivate a Heart of Love

It is possible to love the way God wants us to do it. This is because He can help us transform our hearts and fill us with His love. However, we must be willing to collaborate with the Holy Spirit for this to happen. Do this to enhance God's work in your life.

1. Forgive and Let Go of Hurts:

To keep a heart of love, forgiving offenses and turning over a new page must become your second nature. You can't live in love without forgiving offenses and letting go of your hurts. For instance, if you would stay in your marriage and make a great family, you must learn to forgive. You must be determined to do it several times because your spouse or other family members occasionally offend you. There are three reasons why you must ask God for grace to forgive your spouse or family members:

(1) Jesus Christ has forgiven your sins.

"And be kind to one another, tenderhearted, forgiving one another, just as God in Christ forgave you" (Ephesians 4:32).

Can you imagine what would happen to you if God says He cannot forgive you because of the gravity of your sins? Your portion will be hellfire.

(2) You must forgive to receive God's forgiveness.

"But if you do not forgive men their trespasses, neither will your Father forgive your trespasses" (Matthew 6:15).

(3) Forgiving those who have offended or hurt you is mandatory.

"...even as Christ forgave you, so YOU ALSO MUST DO" (Colossians 3:13).

I don't know what your spouse has done to you; please forgive! I plead with you, forgive!

The devil may present arguments to harden your heart against your decision to forgive. Take note of this: God's position in that matter is that you forgive. Every other idea is not from Him. God can never endorse unforgiveness. Author Marianne Williamson once said, "Unforgiveness, is like drinking poison yourself and waiting for the other person to die." Stop poisoning yourself, forgive! Give your spouse a second chance!

2. **Watch Over Your Heart:**

The seat of love is the heart. The fountain of love flows from our hearts to others through our words and actions. If you desire a heart full of God's love, you must persistently watch against pollutants entering your heart. Proverbs 4:23 counsels,

"Keep your heart with all vigilance, for from it flow the springs of life" (ESV).

Toxic emotions can poison and dry up your fountain of love, rendering you a spiritual misfit. Consider this case. A beautiful lady was approached by a guy who expressed his intention to marry her. The two began an exciting relationship in which the lady poured her love, finances, and everything. One year down the road, the guy dumped her for another lady without any serious cause. This lady became terribly frustrated and bitter. She began blaming everybody; the guy, herself, the person who connected them, even God, who did not stop the man from coming into her life. After a while, another God-fearing and good-looking guy came for her, but she snubbed him; "I don't trust men. They are wicked," she said to herself. The lesson from this short story is that tolerating bitterness will pollute your fountain of love and ruin your relationships, even your destiny. Your relationship with God will be shattered. So, constantly check your heart to root out every toxic emotion before it poisons your soul.

Another reason you must keep checking your heart is that God operates only in love.

"God is love, and whoever abides in love abides in God, and God abides in him" (1 John 4:16).

If you are not in love, you are out of God. So, note that when you switch to hatred, unforgiveness, bitterness, malice, and revenge, you are "On your own," God is not with you. Do all to maintain the bond of peace (Ephesians 4:3). Ensure you abide in love permanently.

3. **Be Willing to Love Like Jesus Christ:**

To have a heart full of love, you must be willing to love like Christ. 1 Corinthians 13:4-8 describes the character of the love of Christ.

"Love is patient and kind. Love is not jealous or boastful or proud 5 or rude. It does not demand its own way. It is not irritable, and it keeps no record of being wronged. 6 It does not

rejoice about injustice but rejoices whenever the truth wins out. 7 Love never gives up, never loses faith, is always hopeful, and endures through every circumstance.

8 Prophecy and speaking in unknown languages and special knowledge will become useless. But love will last forever!" (NLT).

The love described here is supernatural; it surpasses human love. But you can practice it by the power of the Holy Spirit if you are willing.

Asking these two questions constantly will help you express the God-kind of love towards others:
(1) Will I be happy if I am treated the way I am treating this person?
(2) What would Jesus Christ do in this situation? These two questions will check your actions and inspire sacrificial love.

Living at a time when complex conflicts plague all the spheres of our society, ensure that your heart is saturated with the knowledge of God's love. You cannot function in God's will in ignorance. Know to your fingertip what Christ has taught about forgiveness, loving God, loving your family members, fellow believers, strangers, enemies, etc. Then be willing to practice what you are learning.

4. Be Willing to Sacrifice:

The willingness to go the extra mile to add a smile to someone's face is the spirit of sacrifice. Such acts will transform your heart and saturate it with love. Genuine love always demands costly sacrifices. Without sacrifices, what we call love becomes lust. What is "Lust?" It is an intense longing or craving for something that belongs to someone else or a strong sexual desire for someone. This is different from pure love. John 3:16 defines genuine love:

"For GOD SO LOVED the world that HE GAVE HIS ONLY BEGOTTEN SON, that whoever believes in Him should not perish but have everlasting life."

God loved us so much and gave His only Son to save us from sin and make us His children. LOVE gives sacrificially; LUST takes greedily.

Jacob demonstrated genuine love towards Rachel in how he married and lived with her. *"Now Jacob loved Rachel; so he*

> *said, 'I will serve you seven years for Rachel, your younger daughter" (Genesis 29:18).*

How much is the total of your salary in seven years? Let us assume Jacob earned a meager sixty thousand francs ($100). That will be seven hundred and twenty thousand francs ($1,200) in one year and five million and forty thousand francs in seven years ($8,400). How many Cameroonians pay such a massive dowry to marry their wives? Jacob sacrificed those years because he loved Rachel.

True LOVE in marriage is sacrificing to meet your partner's spiritual, emotional, financial, and physical needs. You can only meet your partner's needs when you learn to forget about yourself and go the extra mile to please them. Several women are in pain because the man they live with, who claims to love them, has refused to officialize their marriage. Is your spouse satisfied with the way they are treated? If you genuinely love her, please go and see her parents.

A wife who sincerely loves her husband will not quit because he lost his job or business. Several men have come to me lamenting because their wives became unfaithful, frigid, or unavailable in the home because they had lost their job or business.

You also need the spirit of sacrifice to fulfill your calling in Christ. In Acts 15:25-26, the council in Jerusalem pinpoints Barnabas and Paul as men who sacrificed tremendously for God's work.

> *"Barnabas and Paul, men who have risked their lives for the name of our Lord Jesus Christ."*

Maybe God's call on your life demands great sacrifice to accomplish it. Don't shy away or settle on an easy path. Let God's love in your heart drive you into action. Pay the price to do what God has revealed to you. Go to that rugged terrain to preach the Gospel. Start the work with the little you have. Invest time in prayer and fasting as led by the Lord. Invest that money in God's work. Your reward will be great in this life and eternity.

5. Pursue Unity:

Lovers of unity walk in love. Desiring to live in harmony with others tunes your heart to the frequency of love. Disunity and conflicts are usually the fruits of lovelessness. You can't flow in God's love when you tolerate disunity. Neither can you tell me you love God and, at the same time, encourage division.

We must fervently pursue unity as those who desire to see God's move in our families, churches, communities, and nations. And here are some reasons why:

(1) Unity in diversity is God's will for us. See the nation of Israel – ten tribes working in one country.
(2) There must be unity before the release of God's power (Psalm 133). The Pentecostal revival on the Day of Pentecost was the fruit of unity in prayer (Acts 2).
(3) We are one body. God's church must function as a body, not parts (Ephesians 4:11-16). Apostles, prophets, evangelists, pastors, teachers, and all other spiritual gifts have been released in the church to unite, not divide, build, and not break it. Stop breaking Christ's body in the name of "My ministry."
(4) Unity is the mark of authentic Christianity (John 13:33-34). Division is the trademark of the kingdom of darkness.
(5) Our unity is a witness of the Gospel to the world (1 John 2:9-11).

Beloved in the Lord, we have to fervently pray and work for the unity of the church to survive the onslaught of hell against Christianity. Islamic insurgence, Eastern religions, and LGBTQ are movements whose beliefs vehemently oppose our Christian faith. The days ahead are challenging as these anti-Christ beliefs are gaining ground. Though few, the voice of the LGBTQ community is being heard globally because they are united. Even the Bible emphasizes that there is power and influence in unity. Let us work towards rebuilding broken bridges in the church. As ministers of the Gospel, let us learn to support ourselves in every way possible. Don't join those who think you must bring down somebody to grow. The success of one should be the joy of all.

Most families are also divided and at war with each other. How united is your family? God wants to use you as an agent of reconciliation and reconstruction. If you are willing, He will fill your heart with love and power to do the work for Him.

A Baptism of Love

God demands we should live and work in love. His love engenders peace, joy, and unity. His power to save, heal, deliver, and restore flows where hearts are driven by divine love. Unfortunately, human nature is selfish, greedy, wicked, and prone to division and conflicts. Our sick world needs healing. Only those full of divine love can do it.

Do you desire to walk in God's love? Do you want to be used by God to advance His Kingdom? You need a baptism of love. If you have realized that you need help, sincerely cry out to our Heavenly Father to baptize you with Christ's love. Something will change in your heart.

The baptism of love we need in this season is to be filled with the power to love Christ and His will unto death. The capacity to give ourselves entirely to His cause with a dogged commitment. This ties in with St. Jerome's thought, "Martyrdom does not consist only in dying for one's faith. Martyrdom also consists of serving God with love and purity of heart every day." Ask for a baptism of divine love.

PRAYER POINTS

1. *Father, thank You for this season of revival and restoration.*
2. *Father, thank You for Your move in my family, the Church, and the nation.*
3. *Confess and repent of these sins that are breaking down homes: unfaithfulness, unforgiveness, anger, violence, neglect of marital duties, ungodliness, religion, materialism, etc.*
4. *Confess and repent of these sins that destroy families: idolatry, revenge, wickedness, witchcraft, occultism, immorality, division, competition, alcoholism, gossip, false accusations, etc.*
5. *Confess and repent of these sins that destroy the Church: disobedience, hypocrisy, tribalism, greed, unfaithfulness, corruption, love of money, false teachings, witchcraft, etc.*
6. *Father, have mercy on us and heal us spiritually and physically this season.*
7. *Place your hand on your head and pray 7 times, "Fire of God fall in my heart and destroy anything that wants to take the place of Jesus Christ."*
8. *O Lord, deliver me from every strange fire, in Jesus' name.*
9. *Place your hand on your chest and pray, "Fire of God, fall on me now and purge my tongue from lies-telling and exaggeration, in Jesus' name."*
10. *Fire of God, fall on me now and destroy the power of lust, immorality, and uncleanliness in my soul, in Jesus' name.*
11. *Father, purge our hearts from the love of money, power, and self, in Jesus' name.*
12. *Father, fill the hearts of Your servants with genuine love for Your people.*
13. *Father, cause me to live daily like a living epistle before Your people, in Jesus' name.*

14. *The fire of God burns in my heart now and destroys greed, stinginess, pride, disobedience, and rebellion in Jesus' name.*
15. *You evil spirit assigned to trap me into immorality and sin, be arrested, in Jesus' name.*
16. *Father, I release my heart to You; change it to be what You want.*
17. *Father, give me the heart of Christ, in Jesus' name.*
18. *Lay your hand on your heart and pray 7 times, "Holy Spirit, fill my heart with divine love now, in Jesus' name."*
19. *Father, I receive the power to love what You love and hate what You hate, in Jesus' name.*
20. *Father, I receive the power to love those who hate me, in Jesus' name.*
21. *I receive the fire to love my family members, in Jesus' name.*
22. *Raise your hand and pray 5 times, "Let the garment of divine love clothe me now, in Jesus' name."*
23. *Are there some people you must reconnect with now? Do it immediately.*
24. *Father, let the fountain of divine love open in my heart, in Jesus' name.*
25. *Father, I receive the grace to do for You those things that my flesh hates, in Jesus' name.*
26. *I receive the grace to go where others refuse to go for You in Jesus' name.*
27. *Father, restore in our hearts love for our country, in Jesus' name.*
28. *Father, cause our leaders to love the people they lead in Jesus' name.*
29. *Father, arise and break the powers that are promoting conflicts in this nation and reconcile Your people.*
30. *Father, raise anointed agents of reconciliation to restore peace in war-torn nations across the globe, in Jesus' name.*
31. *Father, pour out Your Spirit in the Church and restore pure love among Christians, in Jesus' name.*
32. *Father, raise agents of unity to restore Christ's body in this land, in Jesus' name.*
33. *I close every door I have opened to the devil through sin or negligence, in Jesus' name.*
34. *I seal every door of my life with the blood of Jesus.*
35. *Wait before God and ask the Holy Spirit to reveal those you must reconcile with. Unforgiveness will keep you in bondage. Forgive them sincerely before you continue.*
36. *I break the yoke of unforgiveness over my life, in Jesus' name.*
37. *Place your hand on your chest and pray 5 times, "I root out every seed of anger and bitterness from my soul, in Jesus' name."*

38. I bind and cast away every evil spirit attached to me because of bitterness against…(mention the name), in Jesus' name.
39. Today, I cancel every claim the spirit of infirmity has over my body and emotions by the blood of Jesus Christ.
40. I now command every spirit of infirmity afflicting me to leave my body, in Jesus' name.
41. Pray 5 times, "Fire of God, fall now and consume every disease in my body, in Jesus' name."
42. Do this 5 times (Open your mouth wide and breathe in deeply, then breathe out fast through your mouth. God's power is healing you right now, in Jesus' name).
43. Father, baptize me with divine love, in Jesus' name.
44. Lord Jesus Christ, teach me how to love others like You love me.
45. Father, pour Your Spirit into marriages, heal and restore them, in Jesus' name.
46. Father, pour out Your Spirit in families, heal and restore them, in Jesus' name.
47. Father, baptize me with fire and make me an agent of peace and reconciliation, in Jesus' name.
48. Father, release Your Spirit and raise agents of reconciliation in families, in Jesus' name.
49. Father, pour Your Spirit upon our youths and draw their hearts to Jesus Christ.
50. Father, I present the members of my household to You now, purge them, and transform their hearts by fire, in Jesus' name.
51. Father, release Your Spirit in the Church and raise ministries for orphans, widows, the poor, street children, and all domains of need.

A Heart Full of Love

Chapter 6
Days 16-18

A Heart Full of Faith

"But the just shall live by his faith" (Habakkuk 2:4)

God moves through people who pursue their Kingdom assignment with steadfast faith. In reality, mighty works are accomplished by the Almighty God through men and women of faith. Unbelief, doubt, fear, and discouragement are vices Satan has used to quench many potential great instruments of revival. God is doing a new work in the hearts of His people this season. I see a mighty army of men and women who fear nothing but sin rising in the land to possess the gates of hell and establish God's Kingdom in the power of the Holy Spirit. Join the move!

He went to Mamfe by Faith

In the 1980s, the leadership of Full Gospel Mission Cameroon considered the Mamfe territory as challenging terrain for the Gospel because the different pastors sent there failed in ministry work. In 1988, Rev Kemamah Solomon Tabu was transferred there as the last trial. The Pastor he would replace called him privately and discouraged him to reject the transfer, promising to mobilize others to back him up. One of his arguments was that his predecessor had lost a son, and he, too, had lost a son in Mamfe. At that time, Rev Kemamah's wife was pregnant with their first son. Rev. Kemamah said, "I didn't sleep the night the transfer was read because I had made a covenant with God to go wherever He sent me. Now I was faced with a difficult decision before me." Early the following day, he met the General Superintendent of the Full Gospel Mission. He told him he was ready to go to Mamfe without his family. The Superintendent, Papa Njemo, encouraged him to go with his family. Trusting God for His power, protection, and provision, Rev. Kemamah went to Mamfe and served there for eleven years with tremendous results.

How it Started

Rev. Kemamah Solomon and his wife, Gladys, arrived in Mamfe with a burning desire to see God reverse the story of His Church in that territory. There were 30 members in the Church. Rev. Kemamah observed,

> "A few of them were committed to the Lord and were prayerful but haunted by fear because of the horrifying spiritual atmosphere of the territory. Heavy witchcraft activity and demonic attacks caused frightening spiritual darkness in the land. Life was very tough for my family because the monthly financial support I was supposed to receive was not coming in."

As soon as they arrived at Mamfe, Rev. Kemamah went to work. To keep himself spiritually fit for the work, he regularly prayed, fasted, and read the Word. To stir spiritual revival in the land, he did three things:

First, he mobilized the Church to pray intensively. He says, "Prayer was the key – persistent all-night prayer programs and long fasts. Not one all-night prayer in a week or one month. We prayed for extended periods. Sometimes we prayed every night for three weeks or more. We started the prayers at 10 pm and closed at 4 am. The impact was awesome."

Second, he trained and involved church members in ministry. He noted,

> "During church service, I would pray for trained members and send them to the pews to lay hands on the people. The possessed would manifest, and the demons would be cast out. People received the baptism of the Holy Spirit. These believers became greatly motivated to work with me. God began using them out of the Church to work wonders."

Third, he organized a mega crusade every year and invited renowned evangelists, mainly from Nigeria, to minister. All these cleared the spiritual atmosphere of the land and ushered in a revival.

The Impact of Fervent Prayer

As Rev. Kemamah and the prayer warriors (Intercessors) continued to pray fervently, God's power began to move and produce noticeable results that attracted people to Christ. Here are some testimonies he recounted:

- *God's power began to move:* "We suddenly began to notice God's move in the Church and the land. Several people began to turn to Jesus Christ. The sick were being healed of diverse diseases and demons cast out. Barren women were receiving children. People began to bring problems from different villages to our Church for prayer. God healed and set them free. These people, who the Lord had visited, invited us to plant churches in their villages. This is how the work spread in Manyu land. Even unbelievers could testify that something was happening in our Church."

- *The fire consumed a bar:* "Most of our prayers occurred at night. One night while we were praying, God opened the eyes of one of the believers, and he saw a huge demon sitting in our Church. While the prayer became too hot, the demon flew away and landed at a bar near our Church. We thought it was just one of those common visions. Surprisingly, the bar caught fire the next morning and was burnt to ashes."

- *A witch doctor escaped for his life:* "A witch doctor lived in a rented house next to our Church. While fervent prayer was going on one night, he picked up a few of his belongings and escaped for his life. He never came back to collect the rest. The landlord began searching for him to come and liberate his house. When he was found, he said, "If I had not left that night, I could have lost my life."

- *A young lady attacked the Pastor:* "God's power moved mightily during the morning service. After the meeting, I went to greet the brethren. Suddenly, a young lady held me by my tie and began to beat me. A young brother rescued me from her. I noticed she was demonized, so I confronted the demons and cast them out. Later, some leaders of the Church said we should discipline her. I refused because she acted under demonic influence."

- ***A witch attacked our prayer warriors' leader:*** "We had prayed with the prayer warriors every night since Monday. On Saturday morning, our prayer warriors' leader, Brother Emmanuel, went to the Mamfe Market to buy something, and a woman who was a notable witch in town openly attacked him. She began to punch and bite the brother. When onlookers asked her why she was doing that, she said, 'These people have spread blood everywhere in this town, and no one can move around freely. Last night they burnt down a pawpaw tree behind my house, and I could not do my work.' She pounced on our brother again and began beating him. The passersby rescued him from her."

A Tussle With the "Mawuh" Cult

The impressive victory of the Church over the "Mawuh cult" in Ebensi village was a significant booster to the spiritual revival that had begun in Manyu land. Some people have testified that the cult has become almost extinct in most localities since then.

In the 1980s and 90s, the "Mawuh cult" was a prominent secret society run by women in most villages in the Manyu area. The communities believed rituals performed by these women would bring fertility and blessings to the land. So, most Manyu villages promoted the cult. Nobody was supposed to be outside nor light a lamp or a torch light when the cult members went out in Eve's attire – stacked naked for their enchantments. In fact, all villagers were supposed to close their doors and turn off their bush lamps as soon as they received the signal that the "Mawuh" women were out for a ceremony. The village council heavily fined defaulters. They also believed a horrific curse would come on those who saw the women during the ritual. To avoid becoming victims, villagers ran helter-skelter to their houses. They shut their doors when they heard the cult members singing and enchanting.

Some "Mawuh" women came to Jesus Christ

At that time, some women who were members of the "Mawuh" group converted and joined the Full Gospel Mission. This was a terrible blow to the cult members, who considered the Church a rival. One night, some church members, including some of the converts from the "Mawuh" cult, were in Church praying with their bush lamps on when the "Mawuh" women came out for a ritual. The believers praying in Church refused to turn off their lights nor stop the prayer because they believed God was supreme and could not be interrupted by a cult.

The following day, the enraged "Mawuh" women went to report the Church to the village council. They accused the Church of despising "Mawuh" and, through their prayers, made it difficult for the spirits to answer them at night. The council immediately summoned and interrogated the church women. The Christian women responded, "If these women claim that "Mawuh" is a goddess, let her arise and defend herself against those who have treated her with disdain. Why should people fight for a god?" Enraged by the Christian women's answer, the village council imposed a severe embargo on them. They were strictly prohibited from going to the village stream to fetch drinking water or bathe, attending the village market, or even going to their farms. The embargo was extended to all Christians of the Full Gospel Mission in that locality.

The following days were agonizing for the Christians and their kids—no water and food for the Christian families. In fact, some of them went for days without taking a bath. Glory be to God; they stood in faith and began to pray fervently. Rev. Kemamah, the District Supervisor in charge of the Church in Ebensi village and his pastoral college, officially reported the matter to the administrators in Mamfe. Surprisingly, there was no response because of administrative bottlenecks. Let me note that one of the sons of the area was the governor of the region at that time and supported the decision of the village council.

The Church responded with prayer and fasting

Seeing that the legal and administrative authorities were nonchalant about the case, Rev. Kemamah called all prayer warriors to

Mamfe for spiritual warfare. Other church members burdened by the problem also joined. So, believers came to Mamfe town from different villages in Manyu for the battle. The Battle plan was to fast without food and water for seven days and pray for divine intervention. If nothing significant happened, the fast would continue with water and no food until God did something. So, they began to fast and cry out to God for intervention. Nothing happened on the first and the second day. On the third day, God's hand showed up. The leading woman of the "Mawuh" cult in Manyu died mysteriously. She was involved in a car accident and died alone while everyone in the vehicle came out safe. The head of "Mawuh" in Ebensi village, where the embargo was imposed, collapsed in her house and died the same day.

The Church had a victory

The authorities of Ebensi villages rushed to Mamfe town immediately to make peace with the Church because they saw clearly that the God of the Church was fighting for His people. They went straight to the chief magistrate and pleaded that he should summon the church leaders for negotiation before the worst should happen. Gendarme officers came to the church compound and took Rev. Kemamah and a few church leaders to the Magistrate's office. He told them they believed God had judged the two women who had died and pleaded something be done fast to avoid more calamities. The village authorities from Ebensi pleaded with the Pastor to stop the fast. After listening to them, Rev. Kemamah told them since the Church had planned to fast for seven days, they should wait for negotiations at the end of the program. The people began to weep and plead, telling the pastors that the Church was free to preach anywhere in the land and that "Mawuh" will never disturb them again. Based on this, Rev. Kemamah told the Christians to stop the fast.

The news of the victory of the Church over "Mawuh" spread in Manyu land like wildfire. Calls began coming from various villages to plant churches for the Full Gospel Mission. Individuals and some councils offered free lands to the Church. "At that time, we had evangelists like the late Philip Ojong, who went from one village to another for evangelistic crusades and church planting programs. Tangible miracles were happening as they preached. Sick people were healed, the possessed delivered, blind eyes opened, and diverse miracles happened. The revival spread in the whole land," commented Rev. Kemamah.

By the time Rev. Kemamah left Mamfe in 1999, the small Church he met with 30 members had planted several churches. The Mamfe District, which had seventy Christians in the first District Convention he organized, had grown into an ecclesiastic area with several local churches, districts, Christians, and pastors.

Faith: Key to God's Power

Faith is the key to receiving and manifesting God's power. Faith is the reason for breakthroughs, miracles, signs, and wonders in our lives. People of faith are more fruitful in the Kingdom than the faithless. The difference between Christians who walk by faith and those who do not is crystal clear.

What is Faith?

Faith is not the product of reason. Hebrews 11:1 gives us an accurate definition of "Faith."

"Now faith is the substance of things hoped for, the evidence of things not seen."

Moffatt's translation of this verse reads,

"Now faith means that we are confident of what we hope for, convinced of what we do not see."

- Faith is the firm conviction that what God has promised you will come to pass without failing.
- Faith is believing that God will do something despite the contrary surrounding evidence.
- Faith is believing in God's promises against all odds.
- Faith is resting on the Word of God and resisting the devil.
- Faith is fully relying on the Word of God. Mary said to Angel Gabriel,
  "Let it be to me according to your word" (Luke 1:38).
- Faith is putting "All your eggs in God's basket." Faith is a risk-taking action when you have every reason not to do so.
- Faith assures you that you have it before it comes to pass.

If you will pray and experience significant supernatural breakthroughs in life and ministry, you need great faith. You can pray and fail, but you cannot pray with faith and fail!

The Just shall live by faith:

We operate in God's Kingdom through the power of faith. Teaching persecuted believers about the role of faith in victorious kingdom living, the author of Hebrews said these about the heroes of old, *"...THROUGH FAITH subdued kingdoms, worked righteousness, obtained promises, stopped the mouths of lions, quenched the violence of fire, escaped the edge of the sword, out of weakness were made strong, became valiant in battle, turned to flight the armies of the aliens" (Hebrews 11:33-34).*

Through this, he affirms that all the victories Gideon, Baraka, Samson, Jephthah, and Samuel exerted over ferocious enemies were achieved by the power of faith and not just the sword. Faith is, therefore, the determining factor to conquering spiritual battles, practicing holiness, walk-in dominion, and enjoying a satisfying long life. Stop trying to devise your methods to fight spiritual battles. It is by faith! For,

"The Just shall live by faith" (Romans 1:17).

Agents of revival are people who live by God's Word. And living by the Word is living by faith.

Nothing Works Without Faith:

Nothing works in the kingdom without faith. Faith is the hand that receives everything that God has to offer you. It is also the hand that releases God's power to rescue the oppressed, lose the bound, and release God's blessings on those in need. That is why Hebrews 11:6 states,

"Without faith, it is impossible to please God..."

In other words, you have no business with God until you switch to the dimension of faith. Unfortunately, most people are stuck at the level of the flesh – human reasoning. Look at this!

- Salvation is impossible without faith! You must believe to be saved.

"By grace, you have been saved through faith" (Ephesians 2:8).

- Receiving healing is impossible without faith! Faith is the miracle connector.

"Your faith has made you well" (Mark 5:34).

- Victory over the powers of darkness is impossible without faith!

"Through faith subdued kingdoms...stopped the mouths of lions" (Hebrew 11:33).

- Nothing is possible without faith.

To seek revival and restoration without firm faith is like trying to call someone on another continent with a telephone without a sim card. Friend, it can't work! Do you know that even God's grace does not work without faith? This means Christianity is worthless without faith – a firm belief in God. Please settle down and build your faith in the Word before you start running around for miracles and breakthroughs.

All Things Are Possible Through Faith:

The Bible makes it abundantly clear that faith can overcome everything. There is no limit to what faith can do. The question is, why are many Christians not experiencing the limitless blessings that faith can produce? Primarily because we have limited ourselves so much to this natural realm. We think and believe only those things that our physical eyes can see. When there is a problem, we quickly turn to man for a solution and only think about God when our effort has failed. Some people don't believe that God can handle certain types of problems. You hear them say, "This one is above the hospital, and even the church cannot handle it; take it to the witch doctors." If that is how you think, you lack faith for a breakthrough.

In Mark 9:14-29, we read the story of the deliverance of a boy possessed by a wicked epileptic demon. The disciples of Jesus Christ tried but could not cast out the demon. He blamed it on their lack of faith and called them "A faithless generation" (vs. 19). This implies they would have cast out the demon if they had the required level of faith. Jesus then turned to the father of the boy and said,

"If you can believe, all things are possible to him who believes" (Mark 9:23).

Faith is an indispensable requirement for the one who needs the miracle and the one ministering. If faith is available, nothing will be impossible for God to do.

How to Cultivate a Heart Full of Faith

Faith is an unwavering belief in God's Word. What you believe will determine the quality of your faith. You may tell me, "I am a Christian." Let me ask you, "What do you believe in?" Some Christians don't believe that a sick person can be healed through prayer and the laying of hands. Such a person can never pray for the sick because of the absence of faith. Still, some pray without expectation because they don't believe God can use them. If you want to become a useful instrument in God's hand, believe this:

1. Believe that Christ lives in you:

The consciousness of Christ's presence in and with you is the foundation of a strong faith. I assume you have repented of your sin, have received Jesus Christ by faith into your heart, and are now following him as a disciple. Now, the Bible tells you in 2 Corinthians 13:5,

"Do you not know yourselves that JESUS CHRIST IS IN YOU?"
Most of God's children lack this conviction – JESUS CHRIST LIVES IN ME.
You must build your faith on this truth – CHRIST LIVES IN ME.

Read this eternal truth:

"Do you not know that YOU ARE GOD'S TEMPLE and that GOD'S SPIRIT DWELLS IN YOU? If anyone destroys God's temple, God will destroy him. For God's temple is holy, and you are that temple" (1 Corinthians 3:16-17).

Child of God, you are God's temple – His very dwelling place. Don't let anyone frighten or intimidate you. Please don't be frightened when agents of darkness talk about their secret societies and cults. You are not their class. You carry God! A cat may look like a leopard, but he should never raise his voice to challenge the leopard. You are the leopard; they are "Pussy cats."

Satan wants to paralyze your faith by causing you to believe that you are empty or inhabited by demons. One day after the baptism of the Holy Spirit in Church, I met a brother who had been filled during the service, looking moody. "Hey, Bro. Marcus, what is wrong with you?" I asked him. "A voice told me an evil spirit filled me during yesterday's service." Was his response. I explained from Luke 11:11-13 that God cannot make him a demon when we ask for the Holy Spirit. Friend, run away from those who keep insisting that there are evil spirits in you. Claim your freedom by reminding the devil that you are God's temple; Christ and the Holy Spirit live in you. Declare that anything that wants to defile you will be destroyed (1 Corinthians 3:16-17).

Those God will use this season to shake the kingdom of darkness as He did with Rev. Kemamah, and the brethren in Mamfe must firmly believe, "CHRIST LIVES IN ME, SATAN, AND HIS AGENTS CAN DO ME NO HARM!"

2. **Believe that You Live in Christ:**

Are you born again? If yes, then YOU LIVE IN CHRIST. Don't try to feel it; believe it! This is fundamental for becoming a man or a woman of faith. You will become a person of great exploits if driven by this conviction: "I LIVE IN CHRIST."

According to the Bible, living in Christ is the most secure location in the world. Colossians 3:3 says,

"...YOUR LIFE IS HID WITH CHRIST IN GOD" (Colossians 3:3).

"I give them eternal life, and they shall never perish; neither shall anyone snatch them out of My hand" (John 10:28).

The expression "In Christ" is commonly used in Paul's Epistles. As a Christian, you cannot understand God's Word correctly nor experience its full power until you prayerfully and in faith accept this biblical truth: "I AM IN CHRIST." You must learn that though you live and walk around like everyone, you live spiritually in Christ.

During the last supper with His disciples, Jesus Christ used the expression more than once. He said that when the Holy Spirit shall be poured out,

"That day you will know that I am in My Father, and you in Me, and I in you" (John 14:20).

And then follows,

"Abide in Me, and I in you...He who abides in Me, and I in him, bears much fruit" (John 15:4-5).

He went on to say,

"If you abide in Me, and My words abide in you, you will ask what you desire, and it shall be done for you" (John 15:7).

You can only take possession of these promises as a Christian once you first accept by faith that you are in Christ.

Paul expressed the same thought in Romans:

"...We were buried with Him through baptism into death" (Romans 6:4).

Romans 8:1 says,

"There is therefore now no condemnation to those who are in Christ Jesus...."

In Ephesians 1:3, Paul wrote that

"God has blessed us with all spiritual blessings in Christ..."

In Colossians 1:28, he says we are

"Perfect in Christ Jesus."

In Colossians 2:6, 10, he says,

"Walk in Him...and you are complete in Him".

Memorize these truths, and let them dominate your spirit. You will develop a strong faith.

Faith is not about joining a church or assuming an ecclesiastical title. It is the quality of what you believe.

3. Believe that Christ is With You:

It is not enough to believe that Christ lives in you. You must also firmly believe that HE IS WITH YOU ALWAYS. You need this mentality to function as a soldier on the cross. If you lack this conviction, you will not confront and conquer the forces of darkness to possess your inheritance. Fear is the consciousness of loneliness or weakness. Imagine how spiritually aggressive you would be if you could convince yourself that Jesus Christ lives in you and is always with you.

Pause for a moment, close your eyes, and picture in your mind this. See the risen Jesus Christ as described by John in Revelation 1:12-16. Visualize His long linen robe, bright white hair, flames of fire oozing from His eyes, His bright face like the sun, fire burning on His feet, seven shining stars in His right hand, and a double-edged sword from His mouth. See yourself standing by Him clothed in a white garment of righteousness. Now, picture a demon or a witch trying to harass you. Just

Jesus' look is enough to send them fleeing. Many believers seem not to know the risen Christ who said,

> *"All authority in heaven and on earth has been given to me. Go therefore and make disciples of all nations... behold, I AM WITH YOU ALWAYS, to the end of the age" (Matthew 28:18-20).*

Jesus Christ is with you ALWAYS! He cannot lie. So, stop shrinking when the Holy Spirit tells you to do something for the Kingdom. Two pastors lost their sons in Mamfe, but the third Pastor succeeded. Why see yourself among the failures? Be optimistic! See yourself as one who will make a difference.

As I write this page, a pastor I don't know called me and explained how he discovered that an unknown person had buried a chicken at the entrance of his Church. He said his Church has stopped growing since then. Another pastor told me how some unknown person frequently defecated at their church door. I asked the man who called me what he intended to do. He said a colleague told him to move the Church to another location. What would you do if you were in his situation? I told him I cannot run away from common witches and wizards. I advised him to mobilize some consecrated men and women to clear out the devils from the territory through night prayers and fasting.

Don't run away from the devil. You will meet him where you think it is safe. Jesus Christ is with you. Stand your ground. Start the fight and see what He will do. He will use you to humiliate the kingdom of darkness and establish His reign, which he has assigned you.

4. Read, Memorize, Mediate, Believe, and Speak the Word:

One who is full of faith is full of the Word. These six practices will help you to fill yourself with the living Word:

(1) *Read:* Eat the Word all the time (1 Timothy 4:13).
(2) *Memorize:* Store it in your mind (Joshua 1:8).
(3) *Meditate:* Chew the Word. Reflect on it with the goal of understanding (Joshua 1:8).
(4) *Believe:* Submit to the Word and let it control you (John 11:40).
(5) *Confess or Declare:* Speak the Word to your situation expecting change (Mark 11:23, Job 22:28).

(6) *Act:* Step out and do what the Word has said; you will be blessed (John 13:17).

So, what should you do when you find yourself in a tight corner, and nothing is working? Go for the Word! Follow the six steps above and see how your faith will explode.

Jesus said,

"For assuredly, I say to you, whoever says to this mountain, 'Be removed and be cast into the sea,' and does not doubt in his heart, but believes that those things he says will be done, HE WILL HAVE WHATEVER HE SAYS" (Mark 11:23).

You can have whatever you say if you say it by faith. You can also ruin your life if you keep saying negative things concerning yourself.

"Death and life are in the power of the tongue, And those who love it will eat its fruit" (Proverbs 18:21).

Are you facing a mountain-like problem in your health, career, ministry, or marriage? Engage God's Word to reverse it! Begin to speak words of faith. A doctor once informed a man with a terminal disease that he had a few weeks to live. He responded firmly and aggressively, "I cannot die in Jesus' name." He stood his ground, and the disease left him alone.

Be Bold!

God wants to accomplish mighty things through you before you leave this world. You are not disadvantaged or incapacitated as long as you are in Christ. You need the mentality of a champion. I love what I read in Judges 5:18 about the tribe of Zebulun.

"Zebulun is a people who jeopardized their lives to the point of death" (Judges 5:18).

God helped them to possess their inheritance because they will never take NO for an answer.

Those who dare to take a risk make history. A coward can never stand out or accomplish anything remarkable because he fears jeopardizing his life. The Bible is replete with men and women who risked their lives to do great exploits with God. Noah built an ark on dry land; at the time, there was no rain on the earth, and he rescued humanity from the great flood (Genesis 2:5). Abraham left his homeland in obedience to God and went to the Promised Land, where out of love for God, he obeyed to sacrifice his son because God told him to (Genesis 22). Esther dared go to the King at the risk of death to request her people's deliverance from annihilation (Esther 7). What about Peter, who dared to step out of the boat and walk on water to go to Jesus while others watched in fear (Matthew 14:29). Apostle Paul made an outstanding commitment to Christ that led to him being used mightily to spread the Gospel to the nations. He testified:

> *"My life is worth nothing to me unless I use it for finishing the work assigned to me by the Lord" (Acts 20:24 NLT).*
>
> *"And I will very gladly spend and be spent for your souls" (2 Corinthians 12:15).*

Is God demanding you take a risk for the Gospel? Obey! He will give you the grace to do His will. Just lay your life as a sacrifice on the altar.

PRAYER POINTS

1. *Father, thank You for saving my soul from hell, in Jesus' name.*
2. *Father, thank You for establishing my feet on the path of truth and life.*
3. *Father, thank You for paying the price on the cross for my freedom.*
4. *Father, thank You because no one can snatch me out of Your hands, in Jesus' name.*
5. *Father, thank You for hiding me in the rock, in Jesus' name.*
6. *Father, thank You because I am complete in Christ.*
7. *Father, thank You because the total price was paid on the cross, and I am free forever, in Jesus' name.*
8. *Father, thank You because I have confessed and erased all the sins forever; Satan has no ground to accuse me anymore.*
9. *Father, thank You for changing my status and identity by making me one with Christ.*
10. *Father, thank You because I have overcome the flesh, the devil, and the world in Christ.*
11. *I receive a clear conscience and the mind of Christ, in Jesus' name.*
12. *I live in Christ and am no longer condemned, in Jesus' name.*
13. *Father, enlighten my understanding to capture divine truth in Jesus' name.*
14. *Father, help those reading this book to understand that we live in Christ and that the devil has no power over us.*

15. Father, like Paul, I bow my knees before You; please teach me this mystery of "Christ in me."
16. Place your hand on your head and pray, "Fire of God, fall on me now and purge my temple, in Jesus' name."
17. I cough out every negative thing in me, spiritual or physical, in the mighty name of Jesus.
18. Take a deep breath through your mouth, then breathe out fast. Do it 5 times.
19. "You will also declare a thing, And it will be established for you" (Job 22:28). Death, disease, and disaster will not prevail against my house, in Jesus' name.
20. "So light will shine on your ways" (Job 22:28). God's light will shine everywhere I go from today, in Jesus' name.
21. "Death and life are in the power of the tongue, And those who love it will eat its fruit" (Proverbs 18:21). Begin to command dead things in your life to resurrect.
22. "When they cast you down, and you say, 'Exaltation will come!'" (Job 22:29). Begin to command your exaltation to manifest, in Jesus' name.
23. Begin to speak blessings over your life, family, and the works of your hands.
24. Father, thank You because today You are filling my heart with supernatural courage to take risks, in Jesus' name.
25. O Lord, open my ears to see beyond the challenges before me now, in Jesus' name.
26. Father, release Your anointing and break anything the devil calls impossible in my life, in Jesus' name.
27. Father, let fear expire in the hearts of those You have called to warn this generation of the coming judgment.
28. I receive fire to do God's will concerning every domain of my life, in Jesus' name.
29. Father, I present myself to You as a living sacrifice, in Jesus' name.
30. Father, I submit my family life to the authority of Your Word and Your will, in Jesus' name.
31. Father, I submit my business and the works of my hands to the authority of Your Word and Your will, in Jesus' name.
32. Father, visit me on this mountain and restore order, in Jesus' name.
33. Father, let Your finger cut off every power of confusion in my home and establish order in this season, in Jesus' name.
34. O Lord, arise and scatter the forces of darkness assigned to scatter our families, in Jesus' name.
35. You enemy of peace, unity, and understanding in my home, be arrested by fire, in Jesus' name.

36. *Father, take over husbands' and wives' hearts and bring them back to the cross for reconciliation, in Jesus' name.*
37. *Father, I declare war against the evil forces of darkness that have been released against my family, in Jesus' name (rebellion of children, laziness, incest, pornography, quarreling, divorce, poverty, accidents, premature death, diseases, anti-Christ, religion, waywardness, etc.).*
38. *You evil spirit responsible for…(mention the name from the list above), be arrested and cast out of my family, in Jesus' name.*
39. *Fire of God, burn in my body, soul, and spirit, and consume to ashes every root of iniquity, in Jesus' name.*
40. *Father, let Your fire fall on my children and break the power of sin that has turned them away from You, in Jesus' name.*
41. *Father, let Your fire fall in families and arrest destiny destroyers of our children, in Jesus' name.*
42. *O Lord, take over the hearts of husbands who have abandoned their families and bring them back home, in Jesus' name.*
43. *O Father, release Your fire, arrest every runaway child who has left home, and bring them back in Jesus' name.*
44. *O Father, release Your fire over every runaway mother who has abandoned her home, and bring them back, in Jesus' name.*
45. *Fire of God, fall now and consume every power of divorce that has risen against the marriages of Your people, in Jesus' name.*
46. *O Lord, take over the hearts of our church leaders and cause them to fear You, in Jesus' name.*
47. *O Lord, restore the fear of God on those who lead in our churches, in Jesus' name.*
48. *Father, deliver the Church from the spirit of religion and restore the Spirit of revival, in Jesus' name.*
49. *Father, those who serve You must be pure; clothe me with a garment of purity, in Jesus' name.*
50. *Father, thank You because You will do mighty things through me from today, in Jesus' name. (Let the Holy Spirit give you more topics).*

Chapter 7
Days 19-21

A Faithful Heart

"I will search for faithful people to be my companions. Only those who are above reproach will be allowed to serve me" (Psalm 101:6 NLT).

There is a quality God is looking for in those He would use mightily in this season; it is faithfulness. In Psalm 101:6, He clearly states that He is looking for people above reproach to serve Him. He is searching for people of integrity, honesty, and loyalty to minister before Him in power. Hence, to run around in God's name with a heart polluted with dishonesty, disloyalty, unfaithfulness, and crookedness is making yourself an instrument in Satan's hands to fight God's work. God is faithful and partners with faithful people to do mighty things on earth. In fact, our call to Christ is a call to a life of faithfulness.

Faithful in Little Things

This famous saying is attributed to Mother Teresa of Calcutta. "Be faithful in small things because it is in them that your strength lies." This summarizes her philosophy of life.

Mother Teresa was born on 26 August 1910. Her family was of Albanian descent. At the age of twelve, she felt strongly the call of God. She knew she had to be a missionary to spread Christ's love. At eighteen, she left her parental home in Skopje. She joined the Sisters of Loreto, an Irish community of nuns with missions in India. After a few months of training in Dublin, she was sent to India, where on 24 May 1931, she took her initial vows as a nun. From 1931 to 1948, she taught at St. Mary's High School in Calcutta. Still, the suffering and poverty she saw outside the convent walls made such a deep impression on her heart that in 1948, she received permission from her superiors to leave the convent school and devote herself to working among the poorest of the poor in the slums of Calcutta. Although she had no funds, she depended on Divine Providence (God's faithfulness). She started an open-air school for slum children. Soon, she was joined by voluntary helpers, and financial support was also forthcoming. This made it possible for her to extend the scope of her work.

On 7 October 1950, Mother Teresa received permission from the Holy See to start her order, "The Missionaries of Charity," whose primary task was to love and care for those persons nobody was prepared to look after. In 1965, the Society became an International Religious Family by a decree of Pope Paul VI. By the 1990s, there were over one million Co-Workers in more than 40 countries.

Mother Teresa's work has been recognized and acclaimed worldwide and has received several awards and distinctions. She served the Lord faithfully and died at age 87 on 5 September 1997, but her legacy lives on.[21]

In her lecture during the presentation of the Nobel Peace Prize to her on 11 December 1979, Mother Teresa shared this testimony: "The other day, I received 15 dollars from a man who has been on his back for twenty years, and the only part that he can move is his right hand. And the only companion that he enjoys is smoking. And he said, 'I have not smoked for one week, and I send you this money.' It must have been a terrible sacrifice for him. But see how beautiful, how he shared, and with that money I bought bread, and I gave to those who were hungry."

Mark O. (12 July 1922 – 7 August 2011), a US Senator, tells of touring Calcutta with Mother Teresa and visiting the so-called "House of

Dying," where sick children were cared for in their last days and the dispensary, where the poor lined up by the hundreds to receive medical attention. Watching Mother Teresa minister to these people, feeding and nursing those left by others to die, Hatfield was overwhelmed by the sheer magnitude of the suffering she and her co-workers faced daily. "How can you bear the load without being crushed?" he asked. Mother Teresa replied, "My dear Senator, I AM NOT CALLED TO BE SUCCESSFUL; I AM CALLED TO BE FAITHFUL."

We are Christ's Stewards

As Christians, we exist to serve Christ. We all have the mandate of Kingdom servants. God expects us to live as Christ's stewards. Unfortunately, stewardship is hardly emphasized in Christian circles these days.

Who is a "Steward?"

A "Steward" in the ancient world was a person who was given the responsibility and authority to rule over the affairs of the household. He functioned as a servant, a waiter, a manager, or a housekeeper for his master. Joseph was a steward in Potiphar's house (Genesis 39). Even though he enjoyed certain privileges, he was a servant; he was not free to go anywhere or do what he wanted without his master's accord.

In Christ, we are stewards of God's grace. This implies two things:

1) *We belong to Christ:*

In Romans 14:8, Paul underlines this truth,

"So, whether we live or die, we belong to the Lord."

In 1 Corinthians 6:19, he emphasizes,

"Do you not know that your bodies are temples of the Holy Spirit, who is in you, whom you have received from God? YOU ARE NOT YOUR OWN; you were bought at a price. Therefore, honor God with your bodies."

We have to allow this scripture to take hold of our hearts. Do you know that as a Christian, you cannot treat or carry around your body the way you like? You cannot use your body anyhow or walk around in public places naked because it makes you feel good. The Holy Spirit sets standards if you are willing to listen.

Before surrendering my life to Christ, I had an uncontrollable passion for jewelry. I wore neck chains, hand chains, and rings. I even fabricated a bronze tooth to decorate my mouth and look good. When the Holy Spirit took over my heart, I felt jewelry was inappropriate. I dumped them and have not worn any jewelry, except my wedding ring since then. Nobody preached to me to throw away my jewelry; the Holy Spirit took away my peace, and I understood He was dealing with my heart. I have never imposed on anyone to do what I did because God deals with each of us differently.

2) *All we have belongs to God:*

All we have comes from Him. He is the owner; we are the keepers or managers.

"For from his fullness we have all received, grace upon grace" (John 1:16).

"What do you have that you did not receive?" (1 Corinthians 4:7).

Having received all from God by grace, Paul points out how we should manage our resources.

"Now, a person who is put in charge as a manager must be faithful" (1 Corinthians 4:2 NLT).

Before learning to manage other people's resources faithfully, God expects you to manage your financial and spiritual resources as a faithful servant of Christ. What does this mean? You are not free to spend your money or use your spiritual gifts however you want. As a young convert, God began to deal with me on how to manage my money. First, I learned to give tithe. I felt 10% was not enough as time passed, so I moved to 20%. I remember how, in those days in the Bible school, I would trek kilometers to fellowship at the evangelistic center in town and back with coins in my pockets. I couldn't use the money because it was God's tithe. God also taught me how to honor him with my first fruits and make sacrifices for His work. At one point, he asked my wife and me to empty our bank account and bring it to the altar. We obeyed. Another time, he asked us to give Him our family car. We did. It was not easy to go without a car for about one year. Remarkably, each time He tested us, we learned a profound spiritual truth about giving and receiving in the kingdom.

Friend, you must consult God to guide you on what to do with your money, time, and spiritual gifts. God is not happy with the way some people mismanage their time. They waste precious time on entertainment and are not productive in the Kingdom. They can spend hours watching TV but are not disciplined enough to read a good book for thirty minutes. God, the owner of all you have, has a plan; you, a faithful manager, should follow it. Others may trade their spiritual gifts to enrich themselves, Not you! Let God guide you on how to package and deliver your ministry. You must not request huge sums of money to go and minister to people. One day, a pastor I was supposed to minister in his church called me to find out how much I expected to receive for the two sessions of ministration. He also asked other questions involving money. I was embarrassed even though I knew that others did it. I told him I don't charge people to minister to them. I don't sell God's grace. You must not copy what celebrities do. Jesus Christ should be your model. Follow His style of ministry. He will show you what to do if your heart is willing to pursue the path of faithfulness.

God rewards faithfulness, not fame!

What is "Faithfulness?"

To be "Faithful" is to be trustworthy and reliable, to be thorough in the performance of one's duty, to be steadfast in allegiance, to be loyal, and to be consistent. To be "Faithful" also means to be steadfast in affection or allegiance to someone. As Merriam-Webster Dictionary puts it, faithful implies "Unswerving adherence to a person or thing or to the oath or promise by which a tie was contracted."

God is faithful:

God is faithful by nature. Our unfaithfulness does not distort his faithfulness.

"If we are faithless, he remains faithful—for he cannot deny himself" (2 Timothy 2:13).

God is faithful to His Word and promises. He will never fail to do what He has promised concerning you. The promise He made concerning the birth of our Savior in Genesis 3:15 was fulfilled after thousands of years.

The promise He made regarding the birth of Isaac was fulfilled after twenty-five years. God is faithful! Psalm 105:8 assures us that He remembers the word He has spoken for a thousand generations. A generation is forty years old. Implying a thousand generations is forty thousand years. God's promise made forty thousand years ago will not fail. The promise of an end-time spiritual revival in the midst of massive apostasy will happen whether we believe it or not (Acts 2:17-19).

If we refuse to repent and align with God for the outpour of His Spirit in our land, He will set us aside and use those who are willing. If this generation is unwilling, He will wait for the next generation. If your denomination is still being prepared, He will use another denomination. Our unfaithfulness cannot stop Him. Our unwillingness and nonchalant attitude cannot demoralize and neutralize His plan.

God expects us to be faithful:

God has wired us in Christ to be faithful. In Galatians 5:22, Paul teaches us that faithfulness is one of the fruits of the Holy Spirit's nature manifested in us.

"The fruit of the Spirit is...faithfulness."

As a Christian, God does not only expect you to have faith in Him; He wants you to be faithful. You should not only believe in Him; you should live for Him. You must be faithful in following Christ, faithful to your spouse, and faithful in doing your work. Above all, God wants you to demonstrate total loyalty in serving those He has appointed over you. For instance, when entrusted with financial responsibility, let there be no story of anything like a missing coin. Do not let anyone suspect you when you are given money to execute an assignment. Never be counted among those who are disobedient, negligent, and rebellious in your organization. Do everything according to the rules and laws in place. You will not prosper in an organization where you refuse to work hard; you curse, criticize, condemn, and disrespect hierarchy. It is better to leave and go where you will serve happily rather than wasting your time cursing the tree feeding you.

The attitude of dishonesty and disloyalty have barred the way to promotion for many people. There are Christians I cannot entrust anything serious into their hands because they have consistently demonstrated an attitude of unfaithfulness.

Hebrews 3:1-2 commends Jesus and Moses for their faithfulness to God.

"Jesus, the apostle and high priest of our confession, WHO WAS FAITHFUL to him who appointed him, just as MOSES ALSO WAS FAITHFUL in all God's house."

God is searching for faithful people to partner with them.

"I will search for faithful people to be my companions" (Psalm 101:6 NLT).

Unfaithfulness, dishonesty, and disloyalty will dissociate you from spiritual alignment, alienating you from God's eternal blessings. Friend, rejecting faithfulness is to deny God's blessings in your life.

"A faithful man will abound with blessings, but whoever hastens to be rich will not go unpunished" (Proverbs 28:20).

If God does not trust you, He cannot entrust anything important into your hands.

Why is Faithfulness Important?

Those unfaithful in their work and disloyal to authority do not understand the blessings of walking in faithfulness at all. Unfaithfulness and disloyalty will disqualify you before God and discredit you before men. Against this backdrop, several people are available but not useable because they are morally bankrupt.

Our faithful God will not commit anything valuable to an unfaithful person in the Kingdom. No human being dares hand his riches to a waster. Let us reflect on why God desires that we walk in faithfulness:

1. Our Faithfulness Reveals God to the World

God is faithful! He does not change (Malachi 3:6). He cannot lie (Numbers 23:19). His promises do not fail (1 Kings 8:56). His ultimate desire is that we should resemble Him in our character. As we saw earlier, faithfulness is so vital to Him that He listed it as one of the fruits of the Holy Spirit in Galatians 5:22. Do you know that your faithfulness in dealing with others reveals God to them? People are blinded to God's truth when a Christian, who should incarnate godliness and integrity, demonstrates unfaithfulness, disloyalty, dishonesty, and rebellion.

As agents of revival, we need hearts filled with the Spirit of faithfulness to represent God in our corrupt world. Without faithfulness, a Christian is not different from an animist or atheist.

2. Faithfulness is a Requirement for Divine Promotion

Promotion comes from God, and faithfulness is the first yardstick. We all desire promotion in career, ministry, business, and from one level of life to the other. Promotion is only guaranteed when you handle your present responsibilities or opportunities effectively. In the parable of talents, Jesus shows us that faithfulness is a key to promotion.

> *"The master was full of praise. 'Well done, my good and faithful servant. You have been faithful in handling this small amount, so now I will give you many more responsibilities. Let's celebrate together!" (Matthew 25:21 NLT).*

Your next level is directly linked to your present faithfulness. Strangely, some people are negligent at their work but desire to be promoted. Will you promote an absentee and dishonest worker in your company to the office of a general manager? An author said, "God has no larger field for one who is not doing his work faithfully where he is." He does not promote unfaithfulness.

3. Faithfulness is a Key to Receiving Our Inheritance in God

God has a glorious inheritance for each one of us in Christ. Our faithfulness to His Word will usher us into it. Abraham, the father of faith, is our example.

> *"You are the LORD God, Who chose Abram, And brought him out of Ur of the Chaldeans, And gave him the name Abraham; YOU FOUND HIS HEART FAITHFUL BEFORE YOU And made a covenant with him To give the land of the Canaanites" (Nehemiah 9:7-8).*

Woah! God found Abraham's heart faithful before Him. He was faithful in following God and in his dealings with people. After risking his life to rescue the people of Sodom, he didn't use that as an opportunity to squeeze money from the king of Sodom and become rich. He told the king,

> *"I would not take a thread or a sandal strap or anything that is yours, lest you should say, 'I have made Abram rich"* *(Genesis 14:23).*

Abraham's riches were clean. Even though he refused to receive corruption money, Genesis 24:1 testifies that he was blessed in everything, just as God had promised him in Genesis 12:2-3. How did you become a millionaire? How did you raise money to build your house or buy the car you drive now? Is it through hard work or crookery? A lady applied for a $8,400 (5.5 million FCFA) grant from the government to run a project. When the money was released, two of her supervisors forcefully curtailed $3,000 (2 million FCFA). She finally received $5,400 (3.5 million FCFA). Stingy and corrupt men and women have contributed to the ruin of our economy.

Be different! Become an agent of change where God has positioned you. I am not interested in what God has not given me. Reject corruption money. Be faithful! Our faithful God will bring you into your inheritance.

4. Faithfulness is a Key to Divine Preservation

God's faithful servants enjoy uncommon divine preservation.

> *"Oh, love the LORD, all you His saints! FOR THE LORD PRESERVES THE FAITHFUL, And fully repays the proud person" (Psalm 31:23).*

Your faithfulness is your Kingdom life insurance policy. Dishonesty and corruption will expose you to destruction. I know a crooked and dubious man who was brutally murdered recently through the settling of scores. Many have died in questionable ways because their wickedness caught up with them.

The faithful enjoy God's security. In a remote village in India, an angry mob gathered around a missionary's house to burn it down. This faithful servant of God and his wife knelt to pray for their security. Suddenly, the crowd began to disperse without touching the house. One member of the church who was in the group to see what the villagers would do later testified that four men in white with flaming swords came down from above and scared the angry crowd away.

No matter how risky your terrain is, get busy serving God faithfully; His angels will continue to preserve you until you finish your assignment.

5. Faithfulness is a Cure for Moral Bankruptcy

Today's society is stinking with moral bankruptcy – dishonesty, deceitfulness, disloyalty, fraud, betrayal, division, falsehood, and corruption. We live in times when fewer people value faithfulness. Most folks are interested in results and care less about how they are achieved. The "Get rich quick" mentality has overtaken many. This is the environment God is calling us to live as "The light of the world" and the "Salt of the earth" (Matthew 5:13-16).

In the days of Prophet Micah, there was a cry expressing the moral decadence of the nation of Israel.

"The godly people have all disappeared; not one honest person is left on the earth.

They are all murderers, setting traps even for their own brothers" (Micah 7:2).

I want you to ask yourself these questions as I ask myself, "What is God saying concerning my standard of honesty, integrity, and loyalty? Am I truthful in my dealings with money? Am I the person people see in public? Will I do better than my corrupt boss if I am allowed to replace them? Am I faithful in little things?" The English writer John Ruskin wrote, "Faithfulness knows no difference between small and great duties."

Psalm 101:6 reveals God's quest for faithful companions to work out transformation in our society.

"I will search for faithful people to be my companions. Only those who are above reproach will be allowed to serve me" (Psalm 101:6 NLT).

The East African Revival (1930s – 1940s) was characterized by a deep remorse for sin, a desire for holiness, a close relationship with God, and treating others with sincere love and honesty. Charles V. Taylor, an Australian Bible scholar and linguist who experienced the revival in Uganda firsthand, explains that there was a fundamental difference between those whose spiritual lives had been revived and others, even other Christians: "Worldly business people would employ 'saved' East Africans in their homes and businesses because they could completely trust them and rely on them to work hard."[22]

How to Cultivate a Faithful Heart

We are born with a corrupt heart prone to lies and unfaithfulness. Becoming truthful and faithful requires collaborating with the Holy Spirit to cultivate such a culture. The following will help you:

1. Value Little Things:

To be faithful, you must cultivate gratitude and celebrate little things. God does great things, but He always starts small. A human being starts as an invisible seed in the womb. A mighty burma tree begins with a minute seed. God started the world with a capital of one man, Adam. If you want to be faithful, humble yourself and begin like Him.

Charles Spurgeon preached to thousands in London every Sunday. Yet, he started his ministry by passing out tracts and teaching a Sunday school class as a teenager. When he began to give short addresses to the Sunday school, God blessed his ministry of the Word. He was invited to preach in obscure places in the countryside, and he used every opportunity to honor the Lord. He was faithful in small things, and God trusted him with the greater things.

Are you faithful in little things? Do you value and protect public property? Have you accepted with joy the new place where God has sent you to now? Don't forget: It is your faithfulness in little things that count before God. He will multiply any little thing you value.

2. Keep Your Word:

To become a faithful believer, you must be determined to keep your word – your promises to God and people. In Psalm 15:1, 4, David presents this as one of the qualities required to dwell in God's presence.

> *"Who may worship in your sanctuary, Lord? Who may enter your presence on your holy hill?...Those who...keep their promises even when it hurts" (NLT).*

Dear friend, sometimes it isn't easy to keep promises because we make them without knowing the future. God demands that you fulfill your promises, even if it hurts you. Don't be a Christian with a double tongue. I know several people who are unreliable. I stare at them when they make promises because they never honor them.

Now, ask yourself, "Do I follow through on my commitments and engagements, or must somebody follow up to fulfill my promises?"

"Do I keep my deadlines?" "Can my spouse or children always rely on me to keep my word?" "Do I keep to time on appointments or bother to call when I am late?"

If you have unfulfilled promises you made to God, go before Him and deal with them. Ask the Holy Spirit to help you. Always pray and listen to the Spirit's voice before making promises. Please make up your mind to keep your word even when it hurts.

3. Focus on the Transformation of Your Heart:

As we mentioned earlier, God transforms our hearts through His Word and the power of the Holy Spirit working with our will. You have to intentionally focus on cultivating a faithful heart.

In the parable of the Sower, the fruitful heart is a good ground. In agriculture, no land is naturally productive without the farmer's labor. So, too, is a man's heart. The heart has to be cultivated to become fruitful. Luke 8:15 gives us four qualities of a fruitful heart:

> *"...the seeds that fell on the good soil represent HONEST, GOOD-HEARTED people who hear God's word, CLING TO IT, and PATIENTLY produce a huge harvest" (NLT).*

1) **Be honest:** When you follow Jesus Christ in honesty, He helps you develop a sincere heart.
2) **Be good-hearted:** When you love the Word and are willing to obey it, God empowers you to practice it.
3) **Cling to it:** When you genuinely love and cling to the Word, God gives you the grace to retain it.
4) **Be patient:** God imparts patience to those willing to do His will at all costs. Without the fruit of patience, you may never experience some of the biblical promises.

Yield your heart to the LORD, let Him transform it, and make it profitable.

4. Watch Over the Gates of your Heart:

Don't allow Satan to enter your heart! There is hope for victory if he fights you from an external position. Judas manifested a high level of disloyalty when he sold Jesus cheaply to the Pharisees and collected thirty pieces of silver. Before the act, the Bible says,

> *"As soon as the bread was in his hand, Satan entered him. 'What you must do,' said Jesus, 'do. Do it and get it over with" (John 13:27).*

Satan found his way into Judas' heart, turning him into a spiritually blind monster who saw only money. How could the man Jesus had selected as an apostle after an all-night prayer and to whom He gave His treasury betray Him? This could happen only to one whose heart has been taken over by the devil.

The stories of betrayal and disloyalty we witness and read daily are baffling. I read the story of teenage twins who murdered their mother. Being raised by a single mother, these girls constantly quarreled with her. One early morning, during a fight, one of them dashed to the kitchen and brought a sharp knife with which they brutally stabbed their mom to death. They dragged her body, dumped it in the bathroom, and left for school as if nothing had happened. Strangely, they pleaded guilty only after four months of a police investigation. The devil had possessed their hearts!

Judas later realized that he had betrayed an innocent man. Still, because Satan had taken over his heart, he committed suicide instead of turning to Jesus Christ, like Peter, for repentance and reconciliation. Satan is after your heart, to possess it. Watch against greed, selfishness, hatred, lies, pride, lust, and covetousness. Protect your heart with love, peace, humility, simplicity, obedience, generosity, patience, etc.

5. **Be Courageous:**

You need courage to do God's will and fulfill your prophetic destiny. It takes courage to obey God fully. Most people compromise standards and become corrupt because of fear.

In Ezra chapter 10, the people of Israel are repenting and lamenting because they had broken God's covenant by marrying strange women. God's will for them was that they send them away. Was it easy to do it? It required divine courage. God gave them because they were willing. In verse four, Ezra told them,

> *"Arise, for this matter is your responsibility. You need to break away from sin and consecrate your life to serve God. We also are with you. Be of good courage, and do it."*

There may be certain things you have to put out of your life to begin to walk in God's ways. Fasting and prayer without radical repentance is a waste of time. Imagine that you are presently living in adultery with someone or owe somebody money and have refused to pay. You are fasting and praying for healing or a breakthrough without dealing with the issue first. God will not listen to your prayer (1 Peter 3:12). Deal with the sin issue before you continue praying.

The good news is that when you step out to do God's will, you can be sure He is with you to defend you.

"Be strong and of good courage, do not fear nor be afraid of them; for the LORD your God, He is the One who goes with you. He will not leave you nor forsake you" (Deuteronomy 31:6).
Courageously step out today and do what God has asked you to do!

Where are Faithful Men and Women?

God is looking for faithful men and women to use as agents of revival. With such people, He will reawaken the consciences of many and bring them to the path of faithfulness and honesty. One day, somebody said, "Forget about integrity. Everybody in this country is corrupt. To have a new Cameroon, all the people from six years must be killed for a new generation to emerge." Was he correct? I disagreed with him and told him that there are people in Cameron who fear God and walk with integrity. I added that I had made up my mind to be different in the midst of the corruption.

It is impossible to live as a faithful disciple of Christ in this world and not face opposition. However, I agree with the person who said, "When faithfulness is most difficult, it is most necessary." If there is a time we need faithful believers for change and Kingdom expansion, it is now. Make up your mind to live as a faithful disciple of Jesus Christ. The Holy Spirit will fill you with the power you need.

PRAYER POINTS
1. *Thank God for teaching you His ways through this book.*
2. *My Father, the God of resurrection, I celebrate You for the victory of Jesus Christ over death.*
3. *Father, thank You for bringing me into the realm of divine truth in Christ.*

4. Father, thank You because in Christ I am more powerful than every witch and wizard, in Jesus' name.
5. Father, I thank You because I rose with Christ and am sitting in heavenly places with Him.
6. Father, thank You for all Your blessings in my life.
7. Father, I believe it is Your will that I make progress in my walk with You and my daily work.
8. Father, thank You because everything You do in my life is perfect.
9. O Lord, open my eyes to see where I have gone back into my past and give me the grace to break out.
10. Have you been faithful in managing your resources and what has been committed into your hands? Ask God to forgive you in any area of negligence.
11. Confess and repent of these sins that ruin relationships: Abuse, unsettled debts, gossip, covetousness, theft, unforgiveness, lies-telling, etc.
12. Confess and repent of these sins that ruin our society: corruption, embezzlement, bribery, unfaithfulness, mismanagement of public funds, tribalism, injustice, cheating, scamming, stealing, falsehood, fraud, etc.
13. What are some of the resolutions you have made concerning making progress with your spiritual life? Pray for grace to do them.
14. Mighty Father, I praise You because You are going ahead of me; my victory is sure, in Jesus' name!
15. Father, thank You for choosing me to be an ambassador of Your Kingdom in this nation.
16. Father, help me not to disappoint You through the attitude of unfaithfulness.
17. Father, arise for the healing of our families, churches, and nation, in Jesus' name.
18. Father, pour Your Spirit and heal our hearts of corruption, embezzlement, bribery, unfaithfulness, mismanagement of public funds, tribalism, injustice, cheating, scamming, stealing, falsehood, fraud, etc.
19. Father, pour Your Spirit and cause us to serve You and man in faithfulness.
20. Father, strengthen me in the inner man to resist every form of temptation to be unfaithful to You, in Jesus' name.
21. Father, teach me how to use my body the way You want, in Jesus' name.
22. Father, teach me how to manage my resources according to Your will in Jesus' name.
23. Father, I receive grace to be faithful in little things, in Jesus' name.
24. Place your hand on your heart and pray 7 times, "Fire of God, fall now and consume the root of unfaithfulness from my heart, in Jesus' name."

25. *Have you been mismanaging money? Pray for grace to establish a good plan.*
26. *Are there debts you must settle? Write down a repayment plan and start reimbursing.*
27. *Check Your house and refund any property you are not supposed to keep.*
28. *Have you instituted a strategy to squeeze money from people in your office and workplace? Put an end to it. Pray for grace to act now.*
29. *Do you have to restitute in any way? Ask for grace to do it now.*
30. *Are you suffering silently because of a secret you have been hiding? Ask for grace to expose it to the right person.*
31. *Father, baptize me with fire to be a faithful manager of public property, in Jesus' name.*
32. *Father, rescue my soul from the seduction of bribery and corruption.*
33. *Fire of God falls in my heart and consumes every seed of fear planted by the devil, in Jesus' name.*
34. Place your hand on your chest and pray, *"I command every strange spirit that has entered my heart to leave now, in Jesus' name."*
35. Place your hand on your heart and pray 5 times, *"O Lion of the tribe of Judah, take over my heart, in Jesus' name."*
36. *I receive supernatural strength to accomplish God's plan concerning me, in Jesus' name.*
37. *Father, restore the Spirit of obedience, faithfulness, and sacrifice in the Church, in Jesus' name.*
38. *I stop every evil power released from hell to stop me, in Jesus' name.*
39. *Dear Holy Spirit, fill and intoxicate me with God's love and lead me through the best way for me, in Jesus' name.*
40. *O Lord, illuminate my heart and help me to grow in the knowledge of the truth.*
41. *Father, shine Your light and reveal glorious things concerning my future, in Jesus' name.*
42. *I cut off every anti-spiritual progress power working against my life, in Jesus' name.*
43. *Father, deliver me from the chains of traditional thinking that block the Gospel, in Jesus' name.*
44. *Father, thank You for calling me to a life of honesty in Christ.*
45. *Father, purge my soul of the poison of dishonesty, in Jesus' name.*
46. *O Lord, vaccinate me with hatred for dishonest gain, in Jesus' name.*
47. *Father, give me the grace to walk in integrity in all I do, in Jesus' name.*
48. *Father, give me victory over the traps of dishonest gains in Jesus' name.*

49. *Father, deliver this nation from the hands of plunderers, in Jesus' name.*
50. *My Father, teach me to be faithful in all financial matters in Jesus' name.*
51. *You spirit of greed and unfaithfulness, lose your grip over my soul in Jesus' name.*
52. *Father, prosper me and wipe out poverty from my family in Jesus' name.*
53. *Father, thank You because You are faithful forever.*

Chapter 8
Days 22-24

A Patient Heart

"Do not become sluggish, but imitate those who through faith and patience inherit the promises" (Hebrews 6:12).

You must cultivate patience if you want to go far with God. It takes the power of patience to learn God's ways, walk in them, and help others know Him. Contrarily, impatience is a destiny destroyer. It will disqualify you from possessing your inheritance in Christ. To quickly get results, some people devise ungodly schemes that ruin their relationship with God. If you genuinely desire to be blessed and used by God, submit to His process and cultivate patience.

God Told me to Wait for my Turn

Sometime in 2006, I went before God with a question that had been bothering me for some time. "Father, why is it that during these ten years I have served as a pastor, I have been inviting several colleagues to preach in my Church, but they do not invite me too? Is it that I am not anointed, or what?" I asked in tears with a broken heart. I had this negative feeling because I felt I was doing my best and deserved to be allowed to visit other churches and minister. I was angry, and a cloud of discouragement overshadowed my heart.

I praise my Heavenly Father, who always speaks to us in moments of confusion and discouragement. His timely words deflated my pride and empowered me to wait my turn patiently. He asked me, "If I send you out now to preach from one city to another or the nations, what message will you take to my people?" My mind quickly scanned, and I discovered I was unfit for such a task. I immediately began to cry to Him, "O Father, have mercy on me; I am presumptuous." He spoke again, "Sit down, let me prepare you." I immediately shrank into my shell.

On that day, it dawned on me that there was a process I had to undergo to be fit for my assignment. It became clear that I was in God's school of preparation for ministry. Furthermore, I understood that I would never attain a certain level of ministry until I patiently went through God's training program. With this understanding, I surrendered to Him and was no longer bothered about receiving invitations to go out for ministry.

I Rejected Opportunities

Just after that encounter, a colleague told me we should travel to Latin America to seek preaching opportunities. He tried to convince me that it would be a lucrative trip, but I declined. Another senior colleague asked me to associate with him so that he could help me start traveling to Europe to preach in churches. I refused to comply. My refusal of those proposals was based on two reasons. First, the feedback I received concerning how they did ministry abroad grieved my spirit, and I wanted to maintain my standards. Second, God had not told me it was time to go out there.

Great doors began to open for me to minister all over Cameroon and beyond when God's time finally came. By God's grace, I have preached in several towns in all the ten regions of Cameroon. I have visited thirteen foreign nations and preached in eleven of them, with powerful results. More doors are opening before me for ministry every day. Presently, I cannot honor all the invitations for ministry that keep coming to me. While writing this chapter, a pastor I don't know in America sent an invitation. He said he had listened to me preaching online and felt he needed me in his Church.

There is a set time to manifest what God has ordained for you. Don't be discouraged by the performances of those presently on stage. Wait for your turn!

You Need Patience

Your preparation to become God's mighty instrument of revival requires time. Also, the promises of God concerning you sometimes need several years to be fulfilled. This explains why you need patience to go along with Him.

What is "Patience?"

Oxford English Dictionary defines "Patience" as "The tolerance of delay or incompetence." Some people don't tolerate delay at all. They want to rush through everything. If you cannot wait, you will waste it!

Others have no business with those who are incompetent. But the scriptures teach us how Jesus picked mere fishermen and patiently groomed them into world-class Apostles. You cannot lead well if you lack patience. The Church needs patient men and women to raise disciples of Christ.

Patience is Steadfastness:

To be patient also means to be steadfast or determined to attain your goal despite opposition, difficulty, or adversity. Impatient people quit their assignments when faced with adversity. A pastor called me one day, "Man of God, I am leaving this church." When I asked why, he responded, "The battles here are too tough for me, and the church is not growing." How many have quit their duty post because they lacked persistence and steadfastness in times of adversity? Agents of revival will not leave where God has assigned them until they see His glory.

Friend, you will never be called a champion if you quit the fight.

Patience is trust:

A common saying is, "The patient dog eats the fattest bone." In other words, you can only get the best in life by exercising patience. Patience with God is trusting and waiting for Him to answer you even when the situation seems impossible. It is the capacity to stay calm and focused in the face of delays, disappointments, challenges, or controversies.

The truth is that those who wait or trust in God never lose in life. They always get the best in God and reveal His glory to the world. There is a miracle on your way; don't give up!

Patience is perseverance:

A patient person bears pains and trials without complaint. A patient fellow is mentally equipped to face the worst to achieve his goal. Complaining, grumbling, surrendering, or compromising is not an option. The ancient Spartan soldiers were outstanding in their combats because they believed one who returned from the battle as a corpse was better than one who returned alive defeated. Paul encouraged his son Timothy to cultivate the endurance of a soldier.

"Therefore endure hardness, as a good soldier of Jesus Christ" (2 Timothy 2:3).

Are you facing attacks, opposition, hardship, or adversity where God has placed you? Don't quit. Ask God for the patience and strength you need to go through the process. You will emerge a winner in Jesus' name.

Why You Need Patience

Often, believers ignore spiritual virtues because they do not understand the blessing of cultivating them. Let us briefly examine why you need to develop a patient heart.

1. You Need Patience to be Fruitful

Even nature teaches us that we need patience to wait for our seeds to grow into plants and produce fruits. Grains of corn planted will yield their fruits after two months and be ready for harvest within three to four months. A kola nut seed planted will need up to ten years or more to bear fruits. Few people in my village grow kola nuts because they take a long time to bear fruit.

In the parable of the Sower, Jesus reveals that we need patience to bear spiritual fruits after receiving God's Word.

"But the seed on good soil stands for those with a noble and good heart, who hear the word, retain it, and through patience by persevering produce a crop" (Luke 8:15).

You will never see results if you cannot patiently apply God's Word in your life. Some want instant results, forgetting that they must persevere in obedience to experience a breakthrough. Before a breakthrough, your persistent obedience must bring you to a critical point where the miracle happens. You will only see it once you engage tenacity.

Some people try to dodge the process, thinking they can get to the top through shortcuts. There is no shortcut to fruitfulness. I read the story of the meeting of President Yoweri Museveni of Uganda and his classmate, who had dropped out of school 65 years earlier to marry. The old man was swimming in poverty with many children. He regretted why he was impatient to finish school like his friend.

As kids, we tried to plant corn like our mothers. Strangely, after sowing, we went out early the next day to dig the grains to see whether they had grown. If you want a fruitful life, submit to the process and avoid shortcuts.

2. You Need Patience to Inherit Good Things

God has beautiful things for you in the future. You must patiently go along with Him through the process to get them.

"He has made everything beautiful in its time" (Ecclesiastes 3:11).

Note the statement "In its time." Everything is beautiful in its time. If you harvest mangoes before time, their taste will be unpleasant. If you buy a car before time, you may borrow money to fuel it. Your business may go bankrupt if you want to build a beautiful house to live in before time. You must do everything following the right time and season, not because you want to impress people.

Apply this counsel,

"Imitate those who through FAITH and PATIENCE inherit what has been promised" (Hebrews 6:12).

Your faith needs patience to inherit the good things God has promised. Abraham followed God patiently and inherited a great family and the Promised Land. Stop running around shopping for prophecies and quick miracles. Patiently follow God's plan for your life; you will inherit the good things He has reserved for you in Christ. I would not be where I am today if I had followed the shortcuts proposed to me by some colleagues years ago.

3. You Need Patience to Pray for Revival

You need patience to pray and experience a move of God in your family, Church, community, or nation. Profound and persistent prayers generate mighty moves of God. Isaiah 32:15 paints the picture of what I am saying.

"Until at last the Spirit is poured out on us from heaven" (NLT).

Somebody must pray "Until at last the Spirit" be poured out in revival. Elijah prayed seven times before the rain came (1 Kings 18:41ff). Our prayers must rise until the clouds are complete for the rain of revival to pour on us.

History reveals that while others were busy complaining about the moral decadence in society, others were seeking God passionately in the place of prayer for the restoration of his holiness, power, and glory. He always answered them.

It is said that Evans Roberts and a group of young men fasted for five years before the fire that sparked the Welsh revival in 1904 fell.

The pastor and Christians of Brownsville Assembly of God Church in Pensacola, Florida, U.S.A, prayed every Sunday evening for revival for more than two years before the fire fell on Father's Day, 28 June 1995.

Charles Finney fasted and prayed for six years before the revival fire fell in 1830.

As we mentioned earlier, William Seymour and Bartleman fasted for almost seven years before the Pentecostal revivals of Azusa Street began on 9 April 1906. Today, we have more than one billion Pentecostals globally.

If we want God's power, then we must be ready to spend time in prayer. It is a known fact that prayerless Christians are powerless. One aspect where the Church is lacking today is prayer. Prayer must be given its rightful place in our personal lives, families, and churches. We must turn away from charlatanism and sincerely seek God for supernatural visitation this season. Only God's power can produce genuine transformation. Let us pray until He comes.

4. You Need Patience to be Steadfast

"Steadfastness" is a word developed by the navy in those days. It meant "To do everything to stay on course despite opposing forces." A Ship on the sea needs the capacity to stay on course despite the storms. Imagine what would happen to the crew if the winds forced the ship with limited food and water supply to take the wrong direction. They will all perish. Another meaning of steadfastness is the ability to retrace the right path when you wander off.

We must develop the capacity to stay on the right path traced by Christ for us. Each of us should also be capable of returning to God's way of holiness when we go astray. In 1 Corinthians 15:58, Apostle Paul admonishes us.

Therefore, my beloved brethren, be steadfast, immovable, always abounding in the work of the Lord, knowing that your labor is not in vain in the Lord."

Also, patience with God will deliver you from risky and costly alternatives. Impatience or lack of steadfastness is responsible for taking shortcuts in life. Unfortunately, shortcuts truncate and ruin destinies. Any project that impatience drives you into will undoubtedly derail, delay, or destroy your destiny. Today, some ladies are lamenting in marriage because impatience led them to marry the wrong man.

Is the devil offering an alternative plan to lure you away from God's plan for your life? Watch out! No matter how attractive it may look, it can never be compared to what God has reserved for you. No matter how wonderful artificial pineapple juice looks, it can never replace fresh-pressed juice. Remember that synthetic can never replace the authentic.

Be patient with God; your reward is sure, and it will be great!

5. You Need Patience to be Approved by God

You need patience to be trained, tried, and approved by God. The impatient cannot go through the training and testing periods successfully. Joseph had received an exciting revelation about his glorious future but was rejected, falsely accused, and abused for several years. He did not give up on his dream. He kept the word. Psalm 105:19 testified about him,

"Until the time that his word came: the word of the LORD tried him."

He patiently waited in trial for the fulfillment of God's Word in His life. In 2 Corinthians 6:4, Paul counsels us to endure hardship patiently.

"In everything we do, we show that we are true ministers of God. We patiently endure troubles and hardships and calamities of every kind" (NLT).

The ability to patiently endure troubles, hardships, and calamities of every kind proves God's grace in our lives. Doing God's will not always be a bed of roses. But His power will always be available to sustain you. When God permits you to go through the fire, He is there with you.

How to Cultivate a Patient Heart

After discussing the critical role of patience in fulfilling your glorious destiny, let us briefly examine some principles you must apply to cultivate a patient heart.

1. Reject the Shortcut Mentality

Somebody said, "Good things take time. Great things take a little longer." This thought will demotivate you if you are plagued by the "Shortcut mentality." People who want quick results at all costs do not appreciate the discipline of waiting for excellent results. However, for the sake of your soul and destiny, carefully consider this truth. Proverbs 13:11 warns us.

"Wealth from get-rich-quick schemes quickly disappears; wealth from hard work grows over time" (NLT).

Every significant work in the Bible took time.

- Noah built the ark for 120 years. It required extraordinary patience to finish it and bring all the animals in. An impatient person would have abandoned it. Above all, he was in the ark for 360 days. What patience!
- Abraham, the father of faith, had Isaac, the seed for the nation of Israel, after waiting for 25 years. An impatient man would have quit trusting God.
- Jesus started His public ministry at 30 years old. He was patient under the authority of His parents until the time assigned for His ministry came (Luke 2:51).
- John the Baptist waited in the wilderness for several years until God introduced him (Luke 1:80). Sensing the

anointing on his life, an impatient man would have hurriedly started his ministry without divine approval.

If you want to work like God, always give the full time required for everything you do. Good things take time. Either you wait, or you settle for less.

2. Develop the Process Mentality

Every genuine work of God must go through a stringent process to produce the desired results. Keep this truth in your mind. Each seed becomes a fruit tree after going through the growth process. If there is any I know, it is a Christmas tree. It is dead but adorned with beautiful colors and borrowed fruits.

Have you received a call from the LORD or a vision to do something great with your life? If yes, then submit to the process of growth for its materialization. Do you know that any product in the market that has not gone through the standard production process is fake? So, refusal to submit to God's procedure for your preparation is a choice for failure or mediocracy.

Driven by a hunger for quick results, some people consult witch doctors for powers to do ministry. The trade of fake certificates is becoming a lucrative business among Christians. It is gross self-deception to buy a certificate you cannot defend or carry around a bogus ecclesiastical title without a mantle.

Follow the process to get the best God has prepared for you in Christ. You will become a tremendous blessing to your generation.

3. Accept Discomfort

One way to develop a patient heart is by accepting discomfort. Paul urges us to exercise patience in affliction (Romans 12:12). James adds that we should be joyful when we are faced with diverse trials,

> *"Knowing this, that the trying of your faith worketh patience" (James 1:3).*

Patience develops when we fully surrender to God's will for us. We find ourselves in situations that can help raise our patience every day. For example, delayed flights, failed promises, traffic congestion, a preacher who preached in Church longer than expected, etc. Also, it could be persecution from enemies of the Gospel or false accusations raised against you. Whatever puts you in a state of discomfort offers an opportunity to develop your patience.

So, amid discomfort, you can stand fast on God's Word in Romans 8:28

"And we know that for those who love God, all things work together for good, for those who are called according to his purpose."

This means that whatever the enemy has planned against you will work for your good. So, don't quickly look for a way of escaping discomfort; listen to the leading of the Holy Spirit on what action to take.

Interestingly, when you suffer wrongfully and bear it patiently, you manifest a Christ-like character to those around you. Such an attitude glorifies God. Jesus Christ, our Master in bearing our sins, suffered wrong from man. He was condemned and crucified without sin (Luke 23:13-18). If we have decided to live like Him, we must be ready sometimes to suffer wrongfully.

Consider every discomfort you face as an opportunity for spiritual training and revealing God's glory.

4. Submit to Spiritual Training

Being aware that God has a training program for you, submit to it. Isaiah 49:2 talks about Jesus' strict preparation process.

"And He has made My mouth like a sharp sword; In the shadow of His hand He has hidden Me, And made Me a polished shaft; In His quiver, He has hidden Me."

If God had to sharpen and polish Jesus Christ before releasing Him at the appointed time to accomplish His ministry, why do you think he has suddenly become impatient to introduce you without preparing you? Your call may be as prophetic and dramatic as those of Moses, Ezekiel, Elisha, and Isaiah. God must prepare you before sending you to minister.

Moses went through forty years of training in the "Sheep University of the Wilderness of Arabia" to become the great leader of Israel. David went through the "University of Tears," pursued daily by King Saul, to become the most outstanding King of Israel.

Let me emphasize that God cannot train you by force; you must be willing. While terrorist leaders recruit people by force and train them to join their militia, Jesus Christ invites us to follow and submit to His training process intentionally.

"Follow Me, and I will make you fishers of men" (Matthew 4:19).

Most people follow Jesus Christ to experience His POWER, but for those who will become His instruments, they must follow Him to know and experience His PERSON.

5. Handle Criticisms Wisely:

As God starts using you to advance His Kingdom, Satan will use some people to fight you. They will hate, criticize, and accuse you falsely. You must handle them wisely for your advantage. I like what this author said: "Difficult people are placed in our path not to defeat us, but develop us." You better say a big AMEN! to that.

There are two kinds of criticisms: (1) Constructive criticism. (2) Destructive criticism. One motivates and boosts your morale; the other demotivates and tears you down. Be wise in responding to unfounded criticism and gossip raised against you. Never waste your time responding to critics who choose to remain in the shadows. They should face you if they are worth it. Instead of investing energy in defending yourself, keep doing the right things. Their lies will become cheap publicity for you. However, it takes patience to do this.

D. L. Moody said this in response to those busy trying to soil his reputation, "If I take care of my character, God will take care of my reputation." You should know this so that you steadfastly focus on your divine assignment regardless of what your detractors say against you.

While you focus on your Kingdom task, pray for your enemies as Jesus recommended.

Bless those who curse you, and pray for those who spitefully use you...and you will be sons of the Most High" (Luke 6:28, 35).

You should pray against the evil spirits using the accuser, but pray for them that God will open their eyes to see your actual picture. Several people have misunderstood my ministry and said horrible things about me. Through prayer, God is opening their eyes to see that Satan was deceiving them to hate me for no reason.

Don't Give up Seeking God

You certainly have promises you trust to see fulfilled in your life, family, ministry, or nation. Maybe you have prayed for a long time without results and feel like giving up. Psalm 103:8 reminds you today of God's unchanging character. He is compassionate, merciful, patient, and faithful.

"The Lord is compassionate and merciful, very patient, and full of faithful love."

He will surely answer you as you patiently and faithfully seek Him.

This is the 22nd year since I started the annual 30-day fast to pray for revival in Cameroon. I have not stopped seeking God for the release of the glory He showed me. Even though the program's multitudes have been saved, delivered, healed, revived, and restored through the program, I am not going to surrender until I see the fullness of His glory in this nation. Romans 8:25 says,

"But if we hope for what we don't see, we wait for it with patience."

I encourage you to seek God with greater determination because you are a great instrument of revival in your family and Church. God has placed this book in your hands to empower you for the task. As we have seen earlier, you will see His glory as He did to those who sought Him sincerely in the past.

Above all, God wants you to be clothed with humility, gentleness, and patience (Ephesians 4:2). These virtues reveal Christ to the world. Jesus Christ wants to use you to reveal Himself mightily to the world around you, plagued by wickedness. Cry out to Him today to clothe you with a garment of patience.

PRAYER POINTS

1. *Father, thank You because You will perfect everything that concerns me.*
2. *Father, thank You because You are with me. I will not be late in life.*
3. *Father, thank You because weeping may tarry for a night, but joy comes in the morning; I will rejoice because my morning has come.*
4. *Father, thank You because those who wait on You will never be put to shame.*
5. *Father, thank You because those who wait on You shall renew their strength; my strength is renewed, in Jesus' name.*

6. *Confess and repent from these sins of impatience: murmuring, complaining, bitterness, rebellion, presumptuousness, lies-telling, compromise, etc.*
7. *Father, cure my heart of impatience, in Jesus' name.*
8. *Place your hand on your heart and pray 5 times, "Every seed of impatience in my life, die now, in Jesus' name."*
9. *I break the power of the shortcut mentality from my mind, in Jesus' name.*
10. *I break the yoke of the fear of failure over my mind, in Jesus' name.*
11. *Father, be merciful and restore me from every error I have made through impatience.*
12. *Father, bring me back to the center of Your will, in Jesus' name.*
13. *I receive the grace to wait for my turn in life, in Jesus' name.*
14. *I receive the grace to go through every process God has for me, in Jesus' name.*
15. *I receive the grace to pay the price for my calling in Jesus' name.*
16. *I receive the baptism of patience to wait for my turn, in Jesus' name.*
17. *I will not die in the wilderness; I must enter my Promised Land, in Jesus' name.*
18. *I refuse to use any shortcut to solve my problem, in Jesus' name.*
19. *I break every power of hell assigned to break me down, in Jesus' name.*
20. *I receive divine strength and renewal in all the areas of my life, in Jesus' name.*
21. *Father, help me discern my seasons of trials so that I will not miss my promotion, in Jesus' name.*
22. *Father, thank You because Your grace will give me victory in every trial, in Jesus' name.*
23. *O Lord, deliver me from bitterness produced in my spirit by difficult trials, in Jesus' name.*
24. *Father, fill me with the patience I need to walk in the Spirit, in Jesus' name.*
25. *Father, thank You because my reward will surely come in Jesus' name.*
26. *Father, help me to patiently endure for my breakthrough like Abraham, in Jesus' name.*
27. *Dear Holy Spirit, take hold of my heart and keep it focused on Jesus Christ.*
28. *I silence any voice of distraction and discouragement from my life in Jesus' name.*
29. *Father, do not allow any person who would turn me away from the path of truth to come into my life, in Jesus' name.*
30. *Father, anoint me with fresh oil and help me to be fruitful in every work I am called to do in Your house, in Jesus' name.*
31. *Father, give me the grace to use all I have to glorify Your name, in Jesus' name.*
32. *Father, remember the brethren who have backslid and bring them back by Your mercy (mention names).*

33. Father, thank You for revealing today the danger of yielding my heart to Satan.
34. Father, hold me back from any step that would open my life to evil spirits, in Jesus' name.
35. I break every stronghold of the devil over my life, in Jesus' name.
36. I receive a baptism of the love of God, patience, peace, and joy, in Jesus' name.
37. Father, move in our families and root out every spirit of anger and violence, in Jesus' name.
38. I will see the end of my problem; it will not see my end, in Jesus' name.
39. My challenges will not break me; they will make me stronger, in Jesus' name.
40. Father, let Your fire fall in families and arrest destiny destroyers of our children, in Jesus' name.
41. O Lord, take over the hearts of husbands who have abandoned their families and bring them back home, in Jesus' name.
42. O Father, release Your fire, arrest every runaway child who has left home, and bring them back in Jesus' name.
43. O Father, release Your fire over every runaway mother who has abandoned her home, and bring them back, in Jesus' name.
44. Fire of God, fall now and consume every power of divorce that has risen against the marriages of Your people, in Jesus' name.
45. O Lord, take over the hearts of our church leaders and cause them to fear You, in Jesus' name.
46. My problems will make me stronger and not break me, in Jesus' name.
47. Begin to proclaim victory over every battle that is going on in your life.
48. Father, give me the grace to focus on the eternal glory ahead of me, not temporal challenges.
49. Father, may You not permit the loss or gain of material things to steal my faith in Christ.
50. Pray for the topics you have written down.

Chapter 9
Days 25-27

A Merciful Heart

"Blessed are the merciful, For they shall obtain mercy"
(Matthew 5:7).

The average human being thinks generally about themselves, ignoring others. The impact of this selfishness and self-centeredness on our society is a proliferation of crimes, conflicts, abuse, oppression, racism, and wickedness. Sadly, those at the bottom of the social ladder suffer the most. Worst still, demonic spirits are tormenting people with strange diseases and problems that need to be addressed. The agonizing cries for deliverance from the spiritually and physically oppressed rise continuously to heaven.

God delivers and restores people through anointed vessels (Nehemiah 9:25-27). Hence, there is an urgent need for men and women whose hearts are fired up with divine mercy and compassion to rise and turn the tides around. These four things always happen when there is a genuine Holy Spirit revival in the Church: (1) Restoration of holiness among God's people. (2) Restoration of zeal for soul-winning, discipleship, and missions. (3) Restoration of God's power for divine healing, deliverance from demonization, miracles, signs and wonders. (4) Restoration of compassion for the suffering in the hearts of God's people. Often, compassion ministries emerge in the Church as a result of the Spirit of mercy that takes hold of believers' hearts.

I have been so blessed today while writing this chapter. A young sister had requested help in a WhatsApp group I am part of, revealing that she had dropped out of school because of persecution. Despite not having money, she expressed her desire to return to school this academic year. A sister in the Lord in the group, moved by compassion, decided to send her back to high school. I was so moved by the amount of money she sacrificed to support someone she had never met.

You need a merciful heart to be useful in God's hands in this season.

God told me, "Be Merciful!"

A remarkable experience significantly changed my life during the annual 30-day fast in October 2014. I was having my quiet time in prayer when God said plainly, "Be merciful!" My heart began racing fast as I tried vainly to connect the instruction to a particular situation. I continued to ponder over the instructions prayerfully during the next three days. Surprisingly, the LORD did not say anything further.

On the fourth day of the fast, we gathered in our Church, Full Gospel Mission Cow Street-Bamenda, Cameroon, for the daily evening prayer session. That evening, I was standing on the platform leading the prayer with my eyes closed when suddenly, I felt the presence of somebody standing before me. I immediately opened my eyes, and to my shock, it was a man I had never met before. He looked furious, and his hand was raised to strike me. Charged in the spirit, I rebuked him thunderously, "Stop it, in Jesus' name!" His hand dropped abruptly like a stone, and he stood still like one hypnotized. I called the ushers caught up in the Spirit of prayer to take him away. I also assigned some church leaders to talk with the man while the program continued. As he was being taken out, I realized the whole place was stinking profusely. You could see people's reactions as they repelled the pungent smell.

At the end of the service, the church leaders I had assigned reported that the man came to beat me up because his girlfriend, whom I didn't know, was attending the program. He had smoked marijuana to fortify himself for the attack. Being a Muslim, he deliberately entered the church hall with a lit stick of cigarette to desecrate our worship place. So, he came to humiliate the Church and beat up their pastor. He confessed to our church leaders that a thing like that cannot happen in a mosque. The perpetrator will be sent to the land of the ancestors.

I was enraged when I heard the report and told the leaders I would deal with the man for insulting us. When I got home after the prayer meeting, I went straight to my place of prayer to call down fire on the man, to teach him a bitter lesson. As I knelt before our Merciful Heavenly Father, I heard Him clearly, "Show him mercy!" I immediately remembered the message ringing in my heart for the last three days. I instantly understood God had been preparing my heart to forgive that man and not destroy him. So, I prayed for him and forgave him.

Something glorious happened the next day. An unknown man and a woman approached me, running as I dropped off the car at the church for the prayer session the following evening. The man asked me, "Can you still remember me?" "No!" I responded. "I am the man who came to the altar to attack you yesterday." He began to plead, asking me to forgive and show him mercy. I assured him that I had forgiven him, but I asked him to attend the service that evening and also asked the Church to forgive him for his unruly attitude before them. He agreed to do so and went into the church hall. I called him up to the front at a point in the service. He pleaded for forgiveness, and the church members forgave him. He said this before leaving the platform: "I pray that God will show me mercy and help me to be like this pastor."

What is Mercy?

"Mercy" is derived from the medieval Latin *'Merced* or *Merces,'* which means "Price paid." It has the connotation of forgiveness, benevolence, and kindness. Mercy is often used in a religious context for giving alms and caring for the sick or the poor.[23]

In the legal sense, mercy often refers to compassionate behavior from a person in power, such as when a judge shows clemency, leniency, or mercy during sentencing.

Finally, mercy is the compassionate treatment of those in distress, especially when punishing or harming them is within one's power. Being merciful is the ability to pity someone in desperate need.

God is Merciful:

God is presented in the Scriptures as eternally merciful to us. *"O give thanks unto the LORD; for he is good: for his mercy endureth forever" (Psalm 136:1 KJV).*

He demonstrates His great mercy:
1) By forgiving our sins when we repent (1 John 1:9).
2) By withholding punishment from us when we cry out to Him for mercy (Joel 2:15-28).
3) By Healing us from diverse diseases and health issues (Isaiah 53:3-5).
4) By liberating His people from suffering and oppression (2 Chronicles 7:13-14).

Jesus Christ is Merciful:

Our Lord Jesus Christ incarnated God's mercy to demonstrate how we should live.

1. Jesus taught mercy:

First, He taught mercy in the context of FORGIVENESS. In Matthew 18:23-35, through the parable of the unforgiving servant, He teaches us to forgive others who need our forgiveness as our Heavenly Father has forgiven us.

Second, He taught mercy in the context of COMPASSION. In Luke 10:30-37, through the parable of the Good Samaritan, He teaches us to show kindness to those we meet in need.

2. Jesus lived mercy:

Because He incarnated mercy in all He did, people cried out to Him for mercy wherever He went. Matthew 9:35-37 records that moved by compassion, unlike the teachers of the Law, He went from one village to another, healing the sick, delivering the possessed, and preaching hope to the poor. The agents of revival needed in this season must incarnate God's mercy.

3. Jesus is our merciful High Priest:

Driven by mercy, Jesus offered his life on the cross for our sins. Today, we have eternal salvation because of His blood shed freely for us.

He ascended to heaven, and as our High priest, He is interceding daily for us.

> *"Consequently, he is able to save to the uttermost those who draw near to God through him, since he always lives to make intercession for them" (Hebrews 7:25).*

Like Jesus, those who would move God's hand this season must be faithful intercessors. They must be driven by compassion and hold God by His Word for divine intervention.

God Expects us to be Merciful:

As those who carry His DNA, our heavenly Father expects us to be merciful to others. Wickedness, callousness, mercilessness, and lovelessness do not reflect God. Here are four reasons why you should become an agent of divine mercy:

5) God has been merciful to you:

You have to show mercy to others because God has been merciful to you. Ephesians 2:4-5 says,

> *"God's mercy is so abundant, and his love for us is so great, that while we were spiritually dead in our disobedience, he brought us to life with Christ. It is by God's grace you have been saved" (GNT).*

God wants us to act in the same way as other people. A merciless believer has lost contact with this truth. Are there some people you must show mercy to? Please ask God for grace to do it.

6) God has commanded you to be merciful:

You cannot live the Christian faith without demonstrating the virtue of mercy. In fact, Christianity without mercy/compassion is like a body without a soul. Micah 6:8 reminds us of three principles of walking with God.

> *"The LORD has told you what is good, and this is what he requires of you: to DO WHAT IS RIGHT, to LOVE MERCY, and to WALK HUMBLY with your God" (NLT).*

Pursue mercy with all your heart.

Ask yourself this question? "Do I treat people with mercy?" Several orphans are languishing out there because of oppression and marginalization. How do you treat those in your family?

7) Show mercy because you need it too:

One way to obtain mercy from God and man is to sow mercy in the lives of others.

James 2:13 says,

> *"You must show mercy to others, or God won't show mercy to you . . . But the person who shows mercy can stand without fear at the judgment" (NCV).*

The mercy you demonstrate towards others will speak for you on judgment day. Every act of mercy and kindness you do is saved in your "Mercy bank." In the day of need, God will open your mercy bank and cause people to favor you. Your children will also enjoy God's mercy and favor with people from your mercy bank.

There is a lot of abuse of power in public offices and the business space. People impose payment for services they are supposed to render freely. A magistrate told us she had a colleague nicknamed "Five hundred thousand." They demanded that amount from all those who came to him with cases. She said one day, a poor widow came with a bundle of money constituted of several old five hundred francs notes. Evidently, she had emptied her savings to seek help from this magistrate for her son. The man collected the bundle shamelessly. I am sick of the torments that we face today in society. Some people throw away files as a way of asking for money. O Lord, have mercy on us!

8) Show mercy because it produces joy:

Showing mercy to others brings happiness. This implies that the more merciful you are, the happier you will be. Proverbs 14:21 says,

> *"If you want to be happy, be kind to the poor; it is a sin to despise anyone" (GNT).*

Nothing can make you happy like wiping the tears of those weeping, clothing the naked, feeding the hungry, defending the voiceless, and making the weak strong. Stingy people lack true happiness. Showing mercy to others is a great secret to happiness; practice it.

Begin in your family. You are going nowhere if you are the only happy person. Those trying to help may not be serious about collaborating with you. Be merciful and continue to educate and help them. God will bless you.

Marks of a Merciful Heart

Our hearts must change when we receive Jesus Christ and begin living in the Holy Spirit's power. These marks are evident in your life if you have a merciful heart.

1) *A merciful person easily forgives those who have fallen:*
   "Make allowance for each other's faults, and forgive anyone who offends you. Remember, the Lord forgave you, so you must forgive others (Colossians 3:13 NLT).

A merciless person refuses to forgive and will not let go of offenses.

2) *A merciful person is patient with people with character flaws:*
   "The wisdom from above is first of all pure. It is also peace loving, gentle at all times, and willing to yield to others. It is full of mercy" (James 3:17 NLT)

A merciless person does not tolerate those with imperfections in character. They brutalize their children because of minor errors. I have seen a parent give a child a "Snake beating" because they broke a drinking glass.

3) *A merciful person helps those who are hurting:*
   "Whenever you possibly can, do good to those who need it" (Proverbs 3:27 GNT).

A merciless person is stingy and does not care about the suffering of those around them.

4) *A merciful person gives a second chance to those who have blundered:*
   "Stop being bitter and angry and mad at others. Don't yell at one another, curse each other, or ever be rude. Instead, be

kind and merciful, and forgive others, just as God forgave you because of Christ"(Ephesians 4:31-32 CEV).

A merciless person closes the door against those who have sinned or made mistakes against them. This is what has ruined some relationships. You must be willing to give a second chance to that person.

Is there someone who needs a second chance from you? Don't hesitate; do it!

5) *A merciful person is kind to their enemies:*
   "Love your enemies! Do good to them. Lend to them without expecting to be repaid. Then your reward from heaven will be very great, and you will truly be acting as children of the Most High, for he is kind to those who are unthankful and wicked. You must be compassionate, just as your Father is compassionate (Luke 6:35-36 NLT).

A merciless person destroys his enemies. God did not destroy us when we were His enemies. Be merciful to those who hate you.

Is there someone who hates you and needs your mercy? Don't hesitate; show them mercy!

6) *A merciful person cares for the lost:*
   "He gave his one and only Son so that everyone who believes in him will not perish but have eternal life" (John 3:16).

A merciless person does not care about those on their way to eternal destruction in hell.

How are you involved in saving the lost and expanding God's kingdom? Get involved now!

7) *A merciful person loves people above money:*
   "You shall love your neighbor as yourself" (Matthew 22:39).

A merciless person values money above people. Today, workers in a company go for months without salaries while the proprietor is living well and creating new businesses for more money.

How do you treat those who serve you? Begin to do it with compassion!

How to Cultivate a Merciful Heart

It is possible to develop a merciful heart. Here are some tips that can help you.

1. Pray for Transformation in your Heart

Prayer generates power for our transformation. This is seen through Jesus' experience at the Mount of Transfiguration. Matthew 17:2 says, as He prayed,

> *"He was transfigured before them, and his face shone like the sun, and his clothes became white as light."*

"He was transfigured" is literally the word *Metamorphoo* – like the English word metamorphosis, which means "To be changed or transformed."

We see that there is a strong link between prayer and transformation.

If you have noticed that your heart is hardened, merciless, unbending, unforgiving, vengeful, prideful, or wicked, it is time to take it before God and pray for a profound transformation. The Holy Spirit will deal with you and give you a soft heart. Remember how I prayed for mercy for three days before the Muslim guy came to attack me in Church? I forgave Him quickly because the Holy Spirit had prepared my heart through prayer.

Also, pray for those hurting you, as Jesus Christ has taught us. This is a way to transform your heart.

2. Teach Yourself

To develop a compassionate heart, you must teach yourself—study on the subject of mercy. Read books on people who invested their lives in helping others. There is no way you would remain indifferent after reading the stories of people like Florence Nightingale, General William Booth, and Mother Teresa, who invested their lives in caring for the suffering.

There are people around you God is using to manifest His mercy and compassion; copy them. You know people who forgave the offenses of their partners for the restoration of their homes; copy them. You know those who have no children but care for several orphans; imitate them. The examples are so many.

You can also partner with a ministry that serves people in need to learn. God will help you if you are willing.

3. Always Remember God's Grace in your Life

Your heart becomes hardened and inhumane when you forget how much God has been merciful to you. Always remember the mercy you have received from God and others, and replicate it to others.

Forgive people promptly when they ask you for forgiveness. I know people who have refused to forgive their offenders, irrespective of the effort made. They say, "Over my dead body, I cannot forgive." You will easily forgive if you think of God's grace manifested towards you through Jesus' death on the cross.

4. Choose to Become a Peace Maker

The society is plagued with violence and conflicts. Marriages are falling apart. Several families live dagger-drawn against each other. Inter-tribal wars are more rampant today. Several nations are at war. The world will indeed know genuine peace only when Jesus Christ returns to establish His reign on earth. In the meantime, God wants us to labor in peace-building.

In Matthew 5:9, Jesus teaches that peacemakers are true Kingdom ambassadors. God may want you to train yourself and establish an organization for peace advocacy.

Maybe your family needs reconciliation and restoration. Turn to God today and ask for grace to become a peace builder among your brothers and sisters. God will anoint and use you to do great things.

5. Start Helping Those in Need

You develop a compassionate heart by going to where people are hurting and helping them. Go to the hospital and visit the intensive care unit. Take a close look at those agonizing in pain. Something will happen to your heart. Compassion swelled in Jesus' heart as He saw the suffering masses. He was moved to help them.

Jesus did not only preach to the sinners; he healed the sick, delivered the possessed, and fed the hungry. He established a perfect example for the Church today. We should not limit the Gospel to preaching, to prepare people for heaven. We must seek divine wisdom to create avenues to solve the physical needs of the people on their way to heaven. God ensured that there was manner for the children of Israel as they journeyed from Egypt to the Promised Land.

I appreciate believers who run orphanages, widow ministries, ministry to street children, ministry to the poor and underprivileged, etc. We need more of such ministries today than in the past.

Set aside part of your income to help those in need. Refuse to be a receiver, no matter your status. Some people erroneously think only those who have much should give. No! You who have little have to give so that God can multiply your seed and bread (2 Corinthians 9:10-11).

Ask For a Merciful Heart

God wants to use you as an agent of revival to reveal His love and power to many people. You need a merciful heart to be that type of instrument. Naturally, the human heart is evil, loveless, and merciless. In this chapter, I have shown you how God can assist you in cultivating a merciful heart.

You must be willing for it to happen. The question is, "Are you willing to release yourself in God's hands to make you the person He wants?" If yes, go before Him now and commit yourself to collaborating with the Holy Spirit to transform your heart. Begin to ask for a merciful heart, and promptly take any step the Holy Spirit wants you to take. Your heart will change!

PRAYER POINTS

1. *Father, thank You for this day and the gifts of mercy available to me.*
2. *Father, thank You for choosing me and marking me with Your name.*
3. *Father, thank You for the gift of Your Word for transforming our hearts.*
4. *Merciful Father, thank You because Your love, mercy, and grace have kept me alive.*
5. *Confess and repent from these sins of mercilessness: Hardheartedness, rebellion, unforgiveness, revenge, violence, abuse, hatred, etc.*
6. *O Lord, I repent for rejecting Your will and following the evil ways of my heart, in Jesus' name.*
7. *Father, deal with any wickedness and foolishness in my heart and give me the correct type of heart I need for an excellent life.*
8. *Father, do a deep work in my heart and make me an agent of peace and reconciliation.*
9. *Lord, release Your purifying waters and purge my heart from wickedness, in Jesus' name.*

10. My Father, take away every stone in my heart and make my heart soft like flesh, in Jesus' name.
11. Place your hand on your heart and pray 7 times, "Fire of God, fall in my heart and consume every seed of wickedness, in Jesus' name."
12. I command every seed of destruction planted by the enemy in any area of my life to burn to ashes, in Jesus' name.
13. Father, baptize me with the Spirit of mercy, in Jesus' name.
14. Take time and pray the above four prayers for family members whose hearts are hardened.
15. Lord, renew me and make me a vessel of honor in the name of Jesus.
16. O Lord, let Your supernatural laser light shine through all the areas of my life and bring total restoration, in Jesus' name.
17. Lord, fertilize my heart and cause me to bear abundant fruits for Your glory, in Jesus' name.
18. Father, thank You for blessing me with appetites for my well-being.
19. Have you been abusing any appetite? Sincerely ask for forgiveness.
20. Are you a victim of any addiction? Cry out to God today for deliverance now.
21. Set rules to protect yourself, and pray, "Father, help me to rule my desire, in Jesus' name."
22. Lay your hand on your belly and pray 5 times, "I command every evil spirit that has attached itself to me through any sin I have committed to leave me now, in Jesus' name."
23. Lay your hand on your head and pray 5 times, "I receive the mind of Christ to walk in purity, in Jesus' name."
24. Father, fill my heart with the knowledge of Your glory, in Jesus' name.
25. Father, pluck my soul into the river of mercy, peace, and thanksgiving in Jesus' name.
26. Identify some people in the place of power in the land who need a heart change. Pray that God will change their hearts.
27. Fire of God, purge my life and make me a vessel of honor for the Master, in Jesus' name.
28. Father, I surrender myself to You; use me the way You want from now, in Jesus' name.
29. Father, let the wind of sanctification blow in the churches in this nation, in Jesus' name.
30. Father, raise a prophetic voice in all the churches to activate revival in Jesus' name.

31. Father, deliver Your servants who have been trapped by greed and compromise, in Jesus' name.
32. Father, have mercy on us for all the bloodshed and wickedness in our land.
33. Father, the hearts of Your people have been turned into hearts of beasts; have mercy and restore them.
34. Father, pour Your Spirit and activate sincere forgiveness in the hearts of those who have been hurt.
35. Father, cause Your Spirit to move and cause reconciliations to begin to happen in families and communities.
36. Father, pour out Your Spirit in the land and restore mercy in our hearts.
37. Father, release Your Spirit and cause enemies to become friends.
38. Mighty Man of war, thank You because You are my Captain and Commander who can never lose a battle.
39. Father, cause those in power to develop compassion for the people, in Jesus' name.
40. Begin to wage war against the spirits causing suffering in the land: rape, assassination, revenge, terrorism, and robbery.
41. Begin to bind these spirits, destroying marriages: abuse, violence, unforgiveness, and unfaithfulness.
42. Begin to lose marriages that are under attack from the grip of Satan.
43. Father, rend the heavens over this nation and pour Your fire against evil kingdoms oppressing Your people.
44. My Father, the God of the Family, be praised forever because You will keep my family strong for the glory of Your name.
45. Father, touch the hearts of spouses who have been hurt and help them to forgive, in Jesus' name.
46. Father, stop that divorce about to take place in the marriages of our loved ones.
47. Father, give us the grace to sacrifice and meet emotional, physical, and financial needs in our marriages, in Jesus' name.
48. Father, teach us to go the extra mile to build our families in Jesus' name.
49. Pray that God will change the hearts of men who want to live with women but are unwilling to marry them.
50. Father, I thank You because You are the giver of every good thing.
51. Father, enlarge my coast financially and make me a generous giver in Jesus' name.
52. Father, arise and shake the kingdoms of the earth for wealth transfer to the righteous in Jesus' name.
53. Father, cause the rain that provokes prosperity to fall on Your people in Jesus' name.

54. Father, preserve and expand the businesses of Your children in Jesus' name.

55. Father, arise and frustrate the evil plan of the wicked to steal the wealth of the nations for global power control, in Jesus' name.

Chapter 10
Days 28-30

A Courageous Heart

"The wicked flee when no one pursues, but the righteous are bold as a lion" (Proverbs 28:1).

We are called to serve God faithfully in a spiritual conflict zone, where the forces of darkness are bent on thwarting every divine purpose concerning us. We are in a battle! Obviously, the powers of hell have truncated the destinies of several chicken-hearted people – those who lack the courage to strike back at him. Oyedepo said, "You need a lion's heart to eat the lion's share." Friend, you can't fold your hands and stroll around nonchalantly as a spectator in the day of war. Casualties will multiply in your camp when you refuse to resist the host of hell in Jesus' name.

God recruits and anoints soldiers of the cross for extraordinary Kingdom activities during revival. I pray that the Holy Spirit will draw you into the army God is raising to do outstanding exploits for the Kingdom. May you receive a courageous heart to put the enemies of your glorious destiny to flight! May you conquer every lost territory and become a genuine agent of revival and restoration where God has established you.

The Courageous Missionary:

David Livingstone (1813-1873) was born in Scotland. He prayed this famous prayer, "God, send me anywhere, only go with me. Lay any burden on me; only sustain me. And sever any tie in my heart, except the tie that binds my heart to Yours." Trained as a medical doctor, he received a call to ministry. He traveled to Africa, where he served as an explorer, medical missionary, and slave abolitionist.

He is also celebrated as one of the best explorers who ever lived. Driven by a passion to open Africa for the Gospel, he risked his life daily to accomplish his dream. Full of courage and tenacity, he traveled over sixty-five thousand kilometers in Africa, mainly on foot and without prior knowledge of what was hidden in the vast land. With his sextant and telescope, Livingstone measured and recorded the position of every village, river, mountain, waterfall, and valley along his way. On his path, he constantly faced lions, crocodiles, cannibals, slave traders, malaria, dysentery, and looming death. Yet, for over thirty years, God led him, protected him, and revealed Africa's deepest secrets to him.

Dependent on divine guidance, Livingstone committed his life to three Cs: Christianity, Civilization, and Commerce. He was convinced that advancing these three objectives would ultimately bring Jesus Christ to the Africans. His letters, books, and journals stirred up public support for the abolition of slavery.

A man sold out to Christ:

David Livingstone, a man sold out to Christ, was determined to succeed at all costs. He wrote this prayer on his sixtieth birthday, 19 March 1873: "My birthday! My Jesus, my King, my Life, my All. I again dedicate my whole self to Thee. Accept me and grant, O gracious Father, that ere this year is gone, I may finish my task. Amen."

His commitment to his work adversely affected his family life. Livingstone spent only four of the seventeen years he was married in the same house with his wife Mary Moffat and children. He regretted later in life that he didn't spend enough time with his children.

"I am immortal till my work is accomplished."

Livingstone once went on an expedition with twenty-seven African workers. His goal was to cross the continent to present-day

Mozambique. They traveled over nine months, encountering dense forests, flooded rivers, crocodile-infested swamps, and wild beasts. At times, he met with friendly natives; other days, he had to pay tribute to savage chiefs to receive safe passage through their lands. But the company was never assaulted!

While at Mozambique, a British captain ready to set sail for England offered David free passage on the "Forerunner" to reunite with his anxious family. But Livingstone would not leave his faithful Makololo workers behind. They would never make it back to Linyanti through hostile tribes and swamplands without his maps. Livingstone gratefully gave the captain letters for his wife Mary and detailed maps of his discoveries for the Royal Geographical Society in England.

Not long after Livingstone had engaged the journey back on foot, a messenger brought the tragic news: "The Forerunner with her cargo and crew had sunk in the Atlantic Ocean." He redrew the maps, rewrote a few letters, and sent them to England. After the supernatural deliverance, Livingstone wrote, "I am immortal till my work is accomplished."

God truly protects those on a mission for Him.

The death of a great hero:

David Livingstone died from dysentery and malaria on 1 May 1873, at 60, in Chief Chitambo's Village in North Rhodesia (now Zambia). He was found dead on his knees, praying to his Lord, who had sustained him on the mission field for over three decades. His faithful servants removed his heart and buried it under a Mvula tree (now the site of the Livingstone Memorial) in Zambia. They dried his body in the sun, bound him in sailcloth, and sealed it with tar. They carried the remains on their heads and walked more than one thousand five hundred kilometers to Bagamoyo to hand it to the British consul there. It took them almost one year to arrive because of the challenges they faced on the way.

The impact of his life:

Though he did little traditional missionary work while alive, Livingstone inspired hundreds of men and women to give their lives for African missions. Mary Slessor, for example, decided to follow in the footsteps of her hero and, in 1875, arrived in Calabar (present-day Nigeria). Peter Cameron Scott, founder of the Africa Inland Mission, was inspired to return to Africa after his first mission failed when he read the inscription on Livingstone's tomb in Westminster Abbey: "Other sheep I have which are not of this fold; them also I must bring."

By 1900, just twenty-seven years after Livingstone's death, the number of Christians in Africa totaled nine million! In 2012, this number reached five hundred million, or 20 percent of the African population. David Livingstone's persistence had indeed opened Africa to the Gospel of Christ. [24]

What is Courage?

The Oxford English Dictionary defines "Courage" as "The ability to do something that frightens you. Also, courage is strength in the face of pain or grief."

Dictionary.com says, "Courage" is "The quality of mind or spirit that enables a person to face difficulty, danger, pain, etc., without fear."

Synonyms of courage are valor, prowess, fearlessness, bravery, audacity, and tenacity.

Courage is not the absence of fear but the ability to subdue fear and forge ahead. A courageous person does not quit until there is victory. David Livingstone did not allow the fear of the terrain or the unknown to deter him from exploring the interior of Africa.

The Lion's Courage:

Male lions have been well known since ancient times as this majestic, regal, and brave animal: a protector, a father, a warrior, and a soldier in its family. Having such an important role as the leader and the defender of the pride, male lions put their bodies on the line to defend everything that is theirs. This means they are ready to fight even when situations are desperate. They can engage in suicide missions like entering the water to fight a crocodile. One male lion, the king of the beasts, can courageously resist a herd of 1,000 gigantic buffalos. Lions are unafraid to hunt animals far bigger than them, like the rhinoceros, giraffe, hippopotamus, elephant, or buffalo. What bravery!

What is a Lion Heart?

Lions are symbols of strength and courage and have been celebrated throughout history for these characteristics. So, "A lion's heart" means a heart full of bravery, courage, a dominant personality, and boldness.

For thousands of years, humans considered lions one of the bravest animals. An ancient Jewish text instructs the faithful to be "As brave as a lion to do the will of your Father in heaven." You need a lion's heart to take possession of your divine inheritance and defend your God-given blessings.

You Need a Lion Heart!

You need a lion's heart to conquer difficult territories, rule among your enemies, and accomplish those tasks that scare others. Without a lion's heart, there are things you will never do, places you will never go, and blessings you will never enjoy in Christ. Proverbs 30:29-30 reveals the tenacity of a lion.

"There are three things which are majestic in pace, Yes, four which are stately in walk. A lion, which is mighty among beasts And DOES NOT TURN AWAY FROM ANY."

Like a lion, David Livingstone forced his way through deadly territories occupied by wild beasts, cannibals, or unyielding warrior kings. It is reported that when he arrived in Scotland after being wounded by a lion, some people could not recognize him. Driven by his divine call, he returned to Africa to continue his mission.

Why You Need a Courageous Heart

As I stated earlier, we have been called to practice our Christian faith in a challenging environment. Maybe you are enjoying relative socio-political peace where you live; you are not spared from the desires of the flesh and worldliness that seek to demotivate you from doing God's will. Therefore, being baptized with the Spirit of courage is imperative to live a victorious life.

1. **You Need Courage to Obey God's Word**

You need a courageous heart to obey God's Word and persevere in His will for your life because your flesh, the devil, and the world will do all to discourage you. In Joshua 1:6-9, God commanded Joshua to be courageous and strong. Verse 8 shows us that God tied courage with obedience.

> *"This Book of the Law shall not depart from your mouth, but you shall meditate on it day and night, so that you may BE CAREFUL TO DO according to all that is written in it."*

As much as he needed courage to dislodge the Canaanites, he had to courageously DO (Obey) all that was written in the Law.

It takes courage to faithfully tithe your income as an investment into God's work. It takes more courage to give your Isaac to God like Abraham. My wife and I needed the courage to give our only car to be sold for building God's house. In fact, we sold the second one and invested half of the money in the same project.

It takes courage to forgive your enemies according to God's Word. Human nature always instigates revenge. I have had to fight against my flesh to forgive those who hurt and abused me to maintain a healthy spiritual life. A brother I led to Christ and baptized insulted and humiliated me publicly on Sunday morning while I stood at the pulpit to introduce a guest speaker.

It takes courage to make restitution. Years ago, God spoke to the late Pa. Njemo, when he was in the Bible School, to confess to a man the sin of adultery he had committed with his wife. His classmates who heard about the revelation told him it was suicidal. The conviction to restitute grew stronger as he fasted and prayed. So, he decided to go. One of his classmates accompanied him. When they got to the man's house, he was shocked to learn that the man had recently surrendered his life to Christ and his wife had confessed the sin to him and obtained forgiveness.

I don't know what area of your life requires total submission to God's will. Be courageous and obey Him. It shall be well with you.

2. You Need Courage to Confront Powers of Darkness

You need courage to confront the powers of darkness in spiritual warfare, deliverance, and destroying idol altars. Jesus said,

> *"Behold, I have given you authority to tread on serpents and scorpions, and over all the power of the enemy, and nothing shall hurt you"* (Luke 10:19).

In Matthew 28:18-19, He assures us that He commands all the powers in heaven and earth. On this backdrop, He commands us to go out and establish His rule on earth without fear. Why do you fear demons, witches, and wizards? It is not because they are powerful but because you are ignorant.

One day, my wife and I were in the house when the most aggressive madman in town jumped in. He dashed against me to strike me. I raised my hand and rebuked him in Jesus' name. He went backward as if a hand pushed him. He launched at me the second time and was repelled by the same force as I kept rebuking him in Jesus' name. He ran out of the house and never tried it again. The Holy Spirit spoke to me as he ran away. "I wanted to teach you that you carry a stronger power than the devil's agents. Fear no man."

By God's grace, we continuously pray and cast out demons from the possessed and oppressed. During a prayer conference we organized in Bafoussam, Cameroon, a family brought a man who was mad and mute, in chains. God's fire came on Him, and he was delivered instantly and began to talk. He asked the sister, "What time is this? What am I doing here?"

In Mark 16:17, Jesus clarifies that every believer can cast out demons.

> *"These signs will accompany those who believe: in my name, they will cast out demons."*

You can cast out demons by exercising your God-given authority in Christ. You may need expertise when dealing with principalities and powers. I challenge you to arise and begin exercising the authority Jesus has given over the forces of darkness that are harassing people around you. Don't assume the position of a toothless bulldog while the devil is ravaging your family.

3. You Need Courage to Confront Evil

You need a courageous heart to confront the evil systems that promote sin and wickedness in your sphere of influence. The event of Jesus expelling the merchants and the money changers from the temple, whom he accused of having transformed God's house of prayer into a den of thieves, was an act of great bravery (John 2:13-17). Jesus defied the temple police, the clergy, and the aristocrats of Jerusalem with a rod of correction. He was driven by a passion to establish the reign of God in the temple. Of this, the Bible says,

"Zeal for Your house has eaten Me up" (John 2:17).

Today, we need men of audacity, like King Asa, to tear down idols and institute divine order in God's house. Prophet Azariah told him God was with him and that he needed to "Take courage" (2 Chronicles 15:2-15.) He bravely removed detestable idols from the land, repaired the Lord's altar near the Temple, and led Israel in worshiping and covenanting with God.

There is a lot of cowardice manifested in the church today. Many Christians easily succumb to new ungodly cultural trends to be accepted in society. Such Christians bring shame to the Gospel. The world needs believers wholly consecrated to Christ—people who fear nothing but sin. We need Bible preachers and writers to confront these evil belief systems polluting the Gospel: materialism, secularism, humanism, and feminism. We need a church that says an emphatic NO against the LGBTQ agenda.

Apostle Jude says,

"I found it necessary to write appealing to you to CONTEND FOR THE FAITH that was once for all delivered to the saints" (Jude 1:3).

Spiritual darkness will engulf the church if we fail to fight to maintain the godly foundation we inherited from our spiritual ancestors. Not everything popular is spiritual. Wake up and confront evil wherever God has positioned you. Ask for wisdom and boldness to dismantle the systems of corruption and oppression instituted where you serve. Don't close your mouth when you are supposed to speak. Take the risk to denounce evil for the liberation of the voiceless; God will defend you.

God will judge you who uses the position of influence He has given you to enrich yourself, ignoring the cries of the oppressed and underprivileged. Every promotion God gives us is for serving people, not enslaving them.

4. You Need Courage to Do Missions

You need courage to go for missions, give for missions, and support missions. Jesus knew that taking the Gospel to the whole world would be daunting, so He assured us that all the powers in heaven and earth were under his authority. He also promised to be with us till the end (Matthew

28:20). Most Christians are not involved in missionary activities because they lack the courage.

We urgently need Christians with the mindset of the Gadites for the expansion of God's Kingdom. Their sons were lion-hearted men who bravely supported David to establish his reign among his enemies.

> *"Some Gadites joined David at the stronghold in the wilderness, mighty men of valor, men trained for battle, who could handle shield and spear, whose faces were like the faces of lions" (1 Chronicles 12:8).*

Talking about their great exploits, the Bible says:

> *"These are the ones who crossed the Jordan in the first month when it had overflowed all its banks; and they put to flight all those in the valleys, to the east and the west" (vs. 15).*

Nothing could stop them from achieving their goal, not even the flooded Jordan or the difficult terrain.

Apostle Paul was a man of this order. In Acts 20:22-24, driven by a burning desire to accomplish God's mission, he defied frightening prophecies that revealed the pain and chains awaiting him and went to Jerusalem. Several localities occupied by the powers of darkness need churches. Somebody must answer the call to go as a missionary.

Young American and European believers answered the call to come and preach in Africa. At the time, this continent was called the "Whiteman's grave." Some came with their luggage in coffins because they knew they could die anytime. Surprisingly, the more they died in Africa, the more young men and women dropped out of school and answered the call to go on missions there.

We Africans owe these missionaries, whose blood was spilled on our soil, a fresh dedication to the cause of world evangelism and missions. The Africans who live in the West have to shine Christ's light and win the lost to pay them back.

There is a need to take the Gospel to the remote areas of Africa and the Islamic nations where millions have never heard about Jesus Christ. Also, multitudes of young boys and girls are trapped in the dungeon of prostitution and hard drugs on our streets, crying out, "Who will deliver me?" Will you go to rescue them? What about the thousands of abandoned street children? Will you go for them?

5. You need Courage to do the Extraordinary

No lasting achievement comes easily. There will be resistance and obstacles to conquer before you attain your extraordinary goal. You may have to endure the misunderstanding of friends and close associates. Above all, if the task is of God, the devil will do everything to discourage you and paint God's promises as unreliable. But in all, you must be audacious and focused to fulfill your destiny.

The story of the deliverance of the children of Israel from Egypt illustrates this truth. After repeated visits to Pharaoh, with a clear demand to free the Hebrews from slavery, all Moses and Aaron got in return was more pain and suffering for their people (Exodus 5). An infuriated Pharaoh commanded his taskmasters to increase the burden on God's people. At this point, Moses developed a feeling of failure as he witnessed the misery of his people. Never define difficulties on your way as a failure. If you do, the enemy of your destiny will take the upper hand.

Your calling came with a promise, and that promise is the spiritual anchor upon which you have to build. Never turn away your eyes from it. God who has made the promise is faithful (Hebrews 10:23). Whenever things become difficult, return to Him and remind Him of what He told you. Also, take note! Those who hate you cannot stop you because the one who gave the promise will defend you. Satan has no power to break God's Word. So, stay focused on God's promise and the assignment He has committed into your hands, in Jesus' name.

How to Develop a Courageous Heart

The courage we are dealing with here is supernatural; it is the work of the Holy Spirit. So, follow these steps to build a courageous and productive life.

1. Be Filled Continuously With the Holy Spirit

The Holy Spirit injects courage and boldness into the believer's heart. Acts 4:31 describes the experience of believers in the early church.

"And when they had prayed, the place they were gathered together was shaken, and they were all filled with the Holy Spirit and continued to speak the word of God with boldness."

To sustain a courageous heart, get baptized in the Holy Spirit and ensure you are always filled. I was timid before, but things changed dramatically when I experienced the baptism of the Holy Spirit. My heart was filled with love, joy, courage, and confidence. God has used me to do things I could not have done by my strength.

Two spiritual exercises that stir courage are; fasting and praying in tongues. Set aside time to charge your spiritual battery through fasting and praying in tongues.

2. Always Remember Your Spiritual Identity

Fear will invade your heart anytime you forget your spiritual identity – who you are in Christ. If you received Christ, then you are righteous in Him (2 Corinthians 5:21). This is your spiritual ID Card:

(1) You are forgiven, delivered, and blessed (Ephesians 1:7; Colossians 1:13; Ephesians 1:3).

(2) Christ lives in you. You live in Him. He is always with you (Colossians 1:27, 3:3; Matthew 28:20).

Two images that describe you spiritually are a Lion and Sheep. The lion speaks of the charisma that should drive you. The sheep speaks of the godly character you should portray. Jesus, the Lion of the Tribe of Judah, lives in you! You are stronger than the enemies of the Gospel fighting against you. You are not a chicken! You are not to be trampled upon by any evil power. So, please do not succumb to their wicked threats!

3. Don't Tolerate Sin

Sin deflates courage; righteousness emboldens the heart. Proverbs 28:1 confirms this.

"The wicked [Sinner] flee when no one pursues, but the righteous are bold as a lion."

In Zechariah 3, the man of God, Joshua, is boldly resisted by Satan because he wore filthy (Sinful) garments. God gave him a change of garment to permit him to minister effectively. Sin will erode your courage to stand before God and shut your voice against the devil. Don't tolerate sin! Often, a sincere believer who has fallen into sin becomes shy, timid, and confused in the presence of their pastor.

4. Read the Stories of Courageous People

Read the biographies of men and women of courage to boost your faith. How did you feel when you read the brief story of David Livingstone at the beginning of this chapter? I have been greatly motivated in my commitment to fulfilling my mission by reading stories of people like Martin Luther, John Wesley, D. L. Moody, Zinzendorf, John Huss, Samuel Morris, Catherine Booth, Florence Nightingale, etc. Leonardo Da Vinci said, "Biographies are templates for a better life." Shape your destiny by reading the biographies of giants in the faith.

Do you have a reading culture? The famous author Mark Twain wrote, "The man who does not read good books is no better than the man who can't."

5. Have a Network of Courageous People

Develop a courageous heart by networking with like-minded people. The principle is we sharpen iron with iron, not wood or plastic (Proverbs 27:17). The people you spend time with will determine the type of spirit you cultivate. For example, suppose your best friend is someone who sees demons behind every dark bush. In that case, they will influence your spiritual perspective. Negative people will poison your mind with fear and discouragement.

Apply the principle of the eagle. Eagles don't fly around with swallows of vultures; they fly with other eagles. So, select eagles – people going far with God and network with them. Eliminate chicken-hearted and faithless people from your inner circle. Jesus sent them away before raising Jairus' daughter from the dead (Mark 5).

There are many battles of the Lord to be fought this season and many territories to conquer for Him. Who will take up the sword of the Spirit and go for the LORD?

Who is on the LORD's Side?

It takes courage to stand on the Lord's side. When Moses cried out to the children of Israel who were worshipping the golden calf at Sinai,

"Who is on the LORD's side? Come to me" (Exodus 32:26).

The Levites responded immediately and turned to him. Moses added,

> *"Thus says the LORD God of Israel, 'Put your sword on your side each of you, and go to and fro from gate to gate throughout the camp, and each of you kill his brother and his companion and his neighbor'" (Exodus 32:27).*

It required outstanding courage for the Levites to raise the sword against their brothers in obedience to God's command.

Friend, we live in the days of God's power – the season of global revival. God is calling on us to arise and do exploits with Him. Answer the call today. Your assignment may be frightening. Don't worry; the Holy Spirit will fill your heart with fire. With God, you will do wonders for the Kingdom, in Jesus' name.

PRAYER POINTS

1. *Father, thank You for choosing me as Your beloved son/daughter in Christ.*
2. *Father, thank You for Your voice that has been working wonders in my life, in Jesus' name.*
3. *Lord Jesus Christ, thank You for Your shepherd voice leading and correcting me.*
4. *Dear Holy Spirit, thank You for Your voice teaching me the deep things of God.*
5. *Father, thank You because You answer prayers; You will answer me in this season.*
6. *Father, I repent from the sin of prayerlessness and spiritual laziness to read and study Your Word, in Jesus' name.*
7. *Father, You have promised that if I seek You with all my heart, I will find You; please show up on my behalf this time, in Jesus' name.*
8. *O Father, as I pray this season, let the angel of supernatural breakthrough visit my family and me in Jesus' name.*
9. *O God of Heaven, visit me this season and open a new page in my life, in Jesus' name.*
10. *Father, strengthen the hands of Pastor Godson and Pastor Anna as they minister to Your people under Your mantle of deliverance, revival, and restoration, in Jesus' name.*
11. *Any evil power behind my trouble, you will know no peace until you release me, in Jesus' name.*
12. *Every evil power prolonging problem, suffering, and bondage in my life and family receive fire and be destroyed utterly, in Jesus' name.*
13. *Anoint yourself and pray this prayer now, "Angel of deliverance and restoration, come now and set me free completely, in Jesus' name."*

14. *Raise your right hand and pray 21 times, "I receive the fire of the Holy Spirit for total freedom, now, in Jesus' name."*
15. *Lay your hand on your belly and pray 14 times, "You evil seed [name the sickness or moving object] in my body, come out now by fire, in Jesus' name.*
16. *Now open your mouth wide, take a deep breath, and cough out (Do it 7 times). Things will come out of your body. Don't stop!*
17. *Father, let Your favor deliver to me what my labor has failed to do, in Jesus' name.*
18. *Father, touch my body with the oil of fruitfulness and terminate any form of barrenness, in Jesus' name.*
19. *Father, let the end of this program mark the beginning of a season of blessings in my life and family in Jesus' name.*
20. *I decree that my stolen blessings should be restored seven-folds, in Jesus' name.*
21. *"Hard-pressed on every side, yet not crushed." The pressures of life will make me stronger and unbreakable in Jesus' name.*
22. *Whatever force that cannot crush Jesus Christ will not destroy me, in Jesus' name.*
23. *"Sometimes, in doubts, but not in despair [Hopeless]." Because the All-knowing God is with me, nothing will cause me to lose my faith in Jesus' name.*
24. *Whether I understand what is happening to me or not, I will not give up my trust in Jesus Christ, in Jesus' name.*
25. *"Persecuted, but not forsaken." Father, because I know that persecution is not rejection, I will not be discouraged and give up, in Jesus' name.*
26. *"Struck down, but not destroyed." Father, because a fall is not a failure, I will bounce back and continue if ever I fall, in Jesus' name.*
27. *Satan, don't waste your time after me; if you knock me down, I will bounce back and continue, in Jesus' name.*
28. *By the power of God's grace, I will succeed where others have failed before, in Jesus' name.*
29. *I reject every spirit of fear and timidity and welcome the Spirit of boldness in my heart, in Jesus' name.*
30. *Because the hand of the Lord is with me, no devil shall prevail against me, in Jesus' name.*
31. *"Behold, the Lord GOD shall come with a strong hand" (Isa. 40:10). Father, come with Your strong hand and crush the evil powers that have been resisting Your glory in my family, in Jesus' name.*
32. *Father, open for me doors that no man can close in my life, in Jesus' name.*

33. Lion of the tribe of Judah, let Your hand be heavy on occultism and witchcraft in this nation, in Jesus' name.
34. O Ancient of Days, arise and make bare Your holy hand in this nation; let all the tribes see Your salvation, in Jesus' name.
35. O arm of the Lion of the tribe of Judah, awake and cut every kingdom that is resisting Your will and purpose for this nation, in the name of Jesus.
36. O right hand of the LORD, strengthen all prayer warriors in the land who are crying out for revival and restoration, in Jesus' name.
37. Every Goliath standing in my way falls now, in Jesus' name.
38. "The LORD is my helper; I will not fear. What can man do to me? Nothing!
39. Fear is banished from my life because the Almighty One of Israel is with me, in Jesus' name.
40. "Because of unbelief, they were broken off, and you stand by faith." Nothing will break me because I am standing on the foundation of faith in Jesus Christ.
41. "We have the same spirit of faith." Because I have the same spirit of faith that inhabited the Apostles, signs and wonders will follow me everywhere I go.
42. "The Lord…afterward destroyed those who did not believe…" I will not perish with the wicked because I have believed in Jesus' name.
43. "That you may know that you have eternal life." Because God's life is in me, I am immortal till I finish my divine assignment, in Jesus' name.
44. "Count it all joy when you fall into various trials." Trials will not break me; they will make me stronger, in Jesus' name.
45. "Blessed is the man who fears the LORD." Because I have chosen the way of the LORD, I am blessed all around, in Jesus' name.
46. "His descendants will be mighty on the earth." My children will excel on the wings of the Almighty God, in Jesus' name.
47. I command the nations to open to the destinies of my children, in Jesus' name.
48. "Wealth and riches will be in his house." My house shall not lack any good thing this year, in Jesus' name.
49. "Surely, he will never be shaken." Because Jesus Christ is in me, only that which can move Him will break me down.
50. "He will not be afraid of evil tidings; His heart is steadfast, trusting in the LORD." This shall be my portion, and that of my loved ones, in Jesus' name.
51. Place your hand on your heart and pray, 7 times, "Spirit of boldness, fall on me, now! In Jesus' name."

52. "No condemnation to those who are in Christ Jesus." Because I have been pardoned and cleansed by the blood of Jesus Christ, no tongue shall be able to condemn or curse me this year, in Jesus' name.
53. "Who do not walk according to the flesh." Because I walk by the Spirit and not the flesh, no spell, no evil injunction, and no spiritual embargo will be able to stop me this year.
54. "The law of the Spirit of life in Christ Jesus has freed me." Because the stronger law is working actively in me, I will enjoy spiritual freedom daily this year, in Jesus' name.
55. Holy Spirit, I bring my mind under Your complete control, now; take full control of my thoughts daily, in Jesus' name.
56. "The Spirit of God dwells in you." Because the Spirit of God dwells in me, I will enjoy a victorious Christian life this year, in Jesus' name.
57. Sin will not rule me because I have been made right with God, and His Spirit gives me life, in Jesus' name.
58. "Spirit of Him who raised Jesus from the dead dwells in you." Because the Holy Spirit dwells in me, I will continue to rise from strength to strength and from glory to glory.
59. "For as many as are led by the Spirit of God, these are sons of God." I declare that I am unbreakable because the Holy Spirit is my Driver.
60. "You did not receive the spirit of bondage again to fear." Lay your hand on your heart and pray 7 times, "You spirit of fear, leave now; Let boldness fill my heart, in Jesus' name."
61. Because I am a joint heir with Christ, whatever He made available to the Church through His death will not lack in my life, in Jesus' name.

Conclusion

Thank God for accompanying you through these thirty days glorious journey with this book. I know the Lord has surely visited and anointed you mightily to be an agent of revival for impact in your family, church, community, nation, and the nations. From now, the anointing will produce extraordinary results in your life as you step out in faith to obey the LORD. I encourage you to cautiously protect God's gracious oil released on your life. Stay away from sin, become an avid reader, meditate daily on the living Word, share the good news with others, become a distributor of God's blessings, practice fasting, and remain heavenly conscious.

Your garment will always be white and your head will never lack oil, in Jesus' name (Ecclesiastes 9:8).

Share your testimonies with us via WhatsApp: (+237) 681.722.404

The Restoration House Project

We are building the RESTORATION HOUSE. It is situated at Tsinga-village, near Olembe Stadium Yaounde – Cameroon. It is a modern complex with a hall of 1,200 seats, offices, a multimedia center, a book publishing house, and a guest house. It will serve as the headquarters of the Christian Restoration Network (CRN), a training center for discipleship, leadership development, ministerial coaching, and the humanitarian activities of CRN, etc.

- Partner with us as we labor to realize this dream for God's Kingdom. For partnership, call: (+237) 674.495.895/ 699.902.618 or WhatsApp: 674.495.895.
- Send your gifts to:
  ECOBANK Acc. No. 0040812604565101
  ORANGE MONEY 696.565.864
  MTN MOBILE MONEY 652.382.693

Endnotes

[1] https://www.biblestudytools.com/bible-study/topical-studies/what-is-a-revival.html (Accessed on 22 June 2023)

[2] https://mycharisma.com/propheticrevival/evangelism2/what-revival-is-not/ (Accessed on 25 June 2023)

[3] https://sbts-wordpress-uploads.s3.amazonaws.com/equip/uploads/2009/09/revival-handout.pdf (Accessed on 22 June, 2023)

[4] https://www.morningstarministries.org/publications/report-revival-africa (Accessed on 25 July 2023)

[5] Denzil R. Miller, *From Azusa to Africa, to the Nations* (Springfield, MO: AIA Publications, 2005), 19-20.

[6] Robert Owens, *"The Azusa Street Revival: The Pentecostal Movement Begins in America."* in The Century of the Holy Spirit: 100 Years of Pentecostal and Charismatic Renewal. Ed., (Vinson Synan. Nashville, TN: Thomas Nelson, Inc., 2001), 56-57.

[7] Frank Bartleman, Azusa Street, (South Plainfield, NJ: Bridge Publishing, Inc., 1980), 58-59.

[8] Owens, 57.

[9] Bartleman, 54.

[10] Miller, 21.

[11] Ibid, 33-36.

[12] Cecil M. Robeck, *The Azusa Street Mission, and Revival* (Nashville, TN: Thomas Nelson, 2006), 7-8.

[13] Estrelda Alexander, *The Women of Azusa Street* (Laurel, MD: The Seymour Press, 2012), 151.

[14] Owens, 48.

[15] Frank Bartleman, *Azusa Street* (South Plainfield: Bridge Publishing Inc., 1980), 41, 58.

[16] Robeck, 91.

[17]https://e360bible.org/blog/the-meaning-of-brokenness-in-the-bible (Accessed 16 August 2023)

[18]Frank Bartleman, *Azusa Street* (South Plainfield: Bridge Publishing Inc., 1980), 41, 58.

[19]Robeck, 91.

[20]https://www.pnas.org PNAS Vol. 103 No. 45 November 7, 2006 Depression induces bone loss through stimulation of the sympathetic nervous system Africa (Accessed on 16 July 2023)

[21]https://www.nobelprize.org/prizes/peace/1979/teresa/biographical (Accessed on 22 August 2023)

[22]New Wineskins Missionary Network, *The Overlooked Revival: The East African Revival Was A Mighty Move of God.* February 2023, https//The Overlooked Revival: The East African Revival Was a Mighty Move of God — New Wineskins Missionary Network

[23]https://www.compassion.com/poverty/mercy-definition.htm# (Accessed on 16 June 2023)

[24]God's Generals: The Missionaries (Nassarawa RD, Kaduna, NIG: Evangel Publishers, 2006), 192-227.

Publications by Christian Restoration Network

1- Prayer Storm Daily Prayer Guide (monthly devotional)
2- Power Must Change Hands Vol.1: Dealing with Evil Foundations
3- Power Must Change Hands Vol.2: Pursue Overtake and Recover All
4- Power Must Change Hands Vol.3: Jesus Christ Must Reign
5- Power Must Change Hands Vol.4: Arise and Shine
6- Power Must Change Hands Vol.5: Family Restoration 1
7- Power Must Change Hands Vol.6: Family Restoration 2
8- Power Must Change Hands Vol.7: Raise an Altar
9- Power Must Change Hands Vol.8: Commanding Total Victory
10- Power Must Change Hands Vol.9: Enjoying Your Freedom in Christ
11- Power Must Change Hands Vol.10: Supernatural Breakthrough
12- Festival of Fire Series No.1: Let the Fire Fall
13- Festival of Fire Series No.2: Anointed Vessels
14- Festival of Fire Series No.3: God's Agent of Revival
15- Dominion
16- Divine Overflow
17- Unbreakable
18- Higher Heights
19- Arresting Family Destroyers 1
20- Arresting Family Destroyers 2
21- Praying Like Jesus
22- Conquering the Giant Called Poverty
23- Generous Living
24- Bind the Strongman
25- Personal and Family Deliverance
26- A Difference by Fire
27- Your Time for Divine Expansion
28- Jesus Our Jubilee
29- The Choice of a Friend
30- Christians and Politics
31- A Dynamic Prayer Life
32- Restoring Broken Foundations

NB: Our publications are in English and French.

For copies, contact your local books store or direct your request to:
Prayer Storm Team
P.O. Box 5018 Nkwen, Bamenda
Tel.: (237) 677.436.964 or 679.465.717 or 675.686.005
godsontnembo@gmail.com

NB: All our books are available in hard copies and soft copies.

Prayer Storm Online Store:
With MTN or Orange Mobile Money *(for those in Cameroon)* and E-Wallet *(for those abroad)*, you can easily obtain the electronic version of this book and other CRN publications via **www.amazon.com** at **https://shorturl.at/pqxyT** or www.christianrestorationnetwork.org/our-bookstore.
https://goo.gl/ktf3rT
Contact (237) 679.465.717 or
prayerstorm@christianrestorationnetwork.org

www.ingramcontent.com/pod-product-compliance
Lightning Source LLC
Chambersburg PA
CBHW061310110426
42742CB00012BA/2123